THE DAWNS OF TRADITION

Published by Nissan Motor Co., Ltd. 1983
Printed in Japan

Contents

JAPAN'S CULTURAL LEGACY

* * *

For sometimes geographical, sometimes political reasons, Japan isolated itself at times in its history. The last and longest period was for two hundred and fifteen years, ending in 1853, when Perry appeared with his "black ships" off Uraga, south of Tokyo. Whether the Japanese liked it or not, those ships opened their nation to an influx of Western culture, thereby changing the course of Japanese history. And it all happened only one hundred and thirty years ago.

In responding to the situation in the 1850s the Japanese had several choices: they could reject the foreign intrusion outright, for instance, ignoring the demands to open the country – and, indeed, some took this approach; or they could warmly welcome Western culture, even if it occasionally meant giving up aspects of their own culture – and some, in turn, took this approach. But the dominant approach lay in between: carefully selecting and importing Western culture, all the while carefully leaving Japanese culture unaffected. I call this the "accretionary approach."

Viewed positively, the accretionary approach accepts foreign culture and absorbs it, while preserving the principal Japanese identity. Viewed negatively, it includes no true appreciation of foreign culture. Misinterpretations and misunderstandings of Western culture were commonplace then, but that bothered no one. One result was that Japan's modernization progressed but its Westernization did not.

Actually, this approach dates well back before the nineteenth century. It is seen often in Japanese history after the sixth century, when the bureaucracy was established. The modern experience merely demonstrated anew that Japanese do not view their culture in terms of it ever ending. To the Japanese, their culture is a kind of continuum, and the foreign influence supplements it but never replaces it.

There was a popular expression, *"wakon yōsai"* ("Japanese spirit, Western learning"), in the 1850s and 1860s, when Western culture was first introduced. In short, Western culture and technology were widely accepted but the Western thinking behind them was not. This approach is a principal reason why during the past century modern science and technology progressed in Japan, but Westernization did not.

Japan is located off the eastern extreme of the Asian continent, and Japanese have only traveled eastward – to the West – in the last hundred years. Historically, they depended almost wholly on visitors to Japan to learn about other cultures.

But the Japanese are naturally inquisitive and they tend not to reject or discard but rather to store and use imported culture. The principal result is that old and new cultural elements, from the East and from the West, coexist in Japan, interacting and often leading to the emergence of new cultural forms.

Let me liken the structure of Japanese culture to the structure of an onion. As the external layers are peeled away, almost nothing remains in the core. The hard core of Japanese culture has brought about the misinterpretations and misunderstandings when foreign cultural elements were brought into Japan, and it has brought about the interacting among cultural borrowings. So the seeming hodgepodge in Japan today is the result of great cultural accumulation and diversification over the centuries around a hard core of indigenous culture.

Some call Japan's cultural hodgepodge total confusion. Others say Japan has no cultural harmony. But I believe Japan's cultural situation is a blend of the old and the new, the East and the West. The blend is like potter's clay for designing new cultural shapes for responding to an ever-changing world. The constant mixing in Japan of things "foreign" and "Japanese" to form new, fresh ideas and lifestyles may in itself be the true cultural legacy of the Japan of yesterday, today and tomorrow.

Teiji

Teiji Itoh

President, Kogakuin University

Editorial Co-Supervisor,
"The Dawns of Tradition"

THE ESSENCE OF JAPANESE CULTURE

* * *

There are many things you can do to try to understand Japan. You can gaze upon a Japanese garden, and see how a refined sensitivity can create its own kind of balance. You can visit the countryside and discover a people at one with nature. You can visit the cities and be appalled by the unplanned jumble. You can live with the Japanese and learn, or rather relearn, the importance of personal relations and group cooperation. You can delve into their religion and philosophy and discover a nation blessedly free of dogma and ideological bias. Or you can simply eat the food, and find not only that small is beautiful but so, too, is that which is simple.

But when you have discovered all these things, there will still be one more thing you want to know: why did the Japanese develop in this unusual way? Are all these things just accident, or are they part of some consistent pattern? Why didn't other people, in particular the nearby Chinese who gave Japan so much of its culture, develop the same way?

To date I doubt if anyone has come up with a convincing answer. And the reason could be quite simple: there is no need for an answer. Almost everything we see in Japan, from the refined sensitivity and the emotionality to the practicality, the jumble, the love of nature and even the complex rules of human relations, is in its essence something instinctive to us all. What the Japanese have done is simply to take this instinctive side of the human personality and refine it to provide the basis of their society. Meanwhile the rest of us for some reason — possibly related to our long histories of conflict with other peoples — have turned to a more intellectual and ideological — a more rationalistic — basis for our existence. We have refined that more rationalistic and non-instinctive side of the personality. The result is our brilliant philosophers, a skill in pure science and abstract theorizing, architecture that is monumental rather than sentimental, design that is studiously symmetrical rather than instinctively balanced, town planning, the ability to argue and debate issues, our strong individualism and so on. These things too have their merits. But they are merits very different from those found in Japan.

It is like the right-hander and the left-hander. Both are the same human being with the same two hands and the ability to use either hand. But some things the right-hander finds easier to do and some things the left-hander is better at. We all have our strong points; there are many things that the non-Japanese peoples do better than the Japanese. But at the more instinctive level — be it the terse sensitivity of the *haiku* or the delightful rhythm of the traditional house — the Japanese often do better than most.

In particular, when it comes to getting people working and making things, the Japanese 'talent' has very real advantages. There is the natural emphasis on group cooperation; you do not work simply to better your own position and prospects. There is the 'simple' pleasure in creating good products. In particular there is the concept of the work unit as the *unmei-kyodotai*, or community with a shared destiny. The enterprise is the expanded family or village. More than anything else it is this instinctive identification with one's place of work, and instinctive sense of responsibility to one's work that explains the remarkable productivity and inventiveness of the Japanese worker. We can learn a lot from it.

Gregory Clark
Professor, Sophia University
(Dept. of Comparative Culture
and Faculty of Economics)

Editorial Co-Supervisor,
"The Dawns of Tradition"

A Destiny Drawn by Nature

Who are the Japanese? And why are they as they are?

Even more than most peoples, the Japanese have been shaped by their environment. From the dawn of their history, close communication and an oftentime precarious coexistence with nature have dominated almost all aspects of the national character and culture.

In this first chapter, we examine a few of the unique natural features of this island nation which have played so important a role in the making of the Japanese.

This is a bird's-eye view of the Japanese archipelago. The "eye" of this "bird" is LANDSAT, the American geophysical satellite cutting an orbital arc 915 kilometers above the earth's surface. Although LANDSAT circles our globe every 103 minutes, it must follow a varying path to maintain its orbit, so it can only photograph the entirety of Japan's island chain once every 18 days. And that doesn't take into account weather conditions. The atmosphere above Japan is noted for its turbulent changes, and the view of the satellite's eye is often obscured by clouds, rain and fog. So this view of Japan is not the result of a single shutter exposure. Rather it took two years to collect the entire composite, and another year to process and transpose its parts using the latest computer technology — a three-year process altogether — to create the map-like image of this nation of nearly 119 million people which appears on our opening page. This image is considered the clearest, most accurate portrayal ever of the ragged chain of islands scattered as a crescent off the east coast of Eurasia proper. In terms of size, these islands are but a footnote to the great land masses opposite. But for the Japanese that footnote is where they have carved out their life and developed their culture.

What environment is responsible for the Japanese culture as we know it today, and for the characteristics and esthetic values of its people? Let's zoom in from this bird's-eye view, closer to the green-mantled slopes and life-giving coastal waters to take a closer look at the nation and its people.

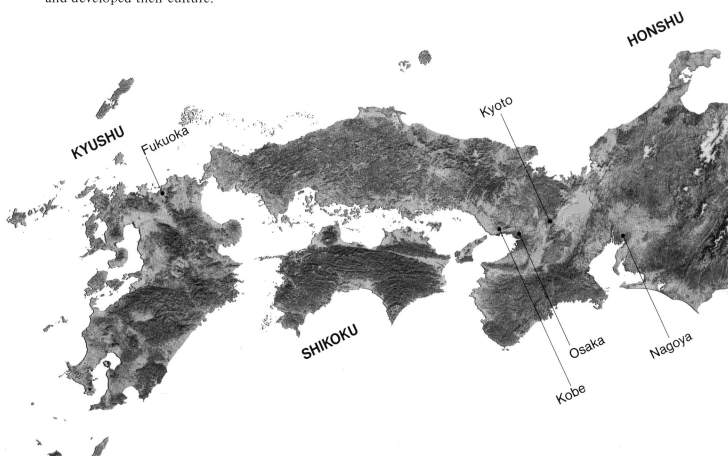

JAPAN SEA

HONSHU

Kyoto

KYUSHU

Fukuoka

SHIKOKU

Osaka

Nagoya

Kobe

HOKKAIDO

Sapporo

PACIFIC OCEAN

Okinawa

TOKYO

Yokohama

A Long, Narrow Archipelago

The total area of the Japan captured by LANDSAT is 378,000 square kilometers — approximately one twenty-fifth the size of the United States of America. This is less, incidentally, than the area of California. Japan is about the same size as Italy, and about half again as large as Chile. It is slightly smaller than Morocco and a shade larger than Malaysia.

The most striking geographical feature of Japan is its length from the northeast to the southwest. Curving along a narrow bow paralleling the coast of the Asian mainland, Japan

Notoro Point, Abashiri, Hokkaido.

Moon over Abashiri.

Hokkaido farmland.

Hiji River in Shikoku.

Biwa Lake near Kyoto.

stretches almost 3,000 kilometers from its southernmost island to its northern tip.

This geographical reach is unusually broad for such a relatively small nation: latitude is from 46 degrees north to 24 degrees north. If an image of Japan were superimposed upon a map of the North American continent, the northern tip of Japan would lie at Montreal, Canada, and the southern extremity slightly south of Houston, Texas. Applying the same test to another side of the world, the northernmost point is Vienna, Austria, and in the middle of the Sahara Desert in the south.

The area figures alone do not yield a truly accurate image of the long, narrow curve along which the islands of Japan are clustered. There are four main islands. They are Hokkaido, to the north, while to the south lie the largest, Honshu, (the location of the national capital, Tokyo), Shikoku and Kyushu in that geographical order. But on all sides and between these four major island "mainlands" are over 3,000 smaller islands – and the coasts of the four main islands appear as a strip of torn and frayed calico.

According to Japanese mythology, as compiled in the epic *Kojiki,* the Japanese Islands were created by the god Izanagi and the goddess Izanami. The legend says the couple perched atop the "floating bridge of heaven," and stirred the ocean with a holy sword received from Amatsukami, the God of Heaven. When the two deities raised the sword from the waters, ocean salt dripped from the tip of the weapon, fell back to the ocean, and accumulated to form the isle of Onogoro. Izanagi and Izanami then descended to this island, married, and gave birth to island upon island until the archipelago was complete. The storytellers of ancient times who passed this myth on from generation to generation undoubtedly based their tale on how they imagined the Japanese island chain would appear to the human eye if viewed from high in the heavens.

The Japanese dwell in a dynamic and ever-shifting, even if restricted, natural setting, from cold northern seas to tepid southern waters. Although they are now thought of as a single people, there are striking dissimilarities in geography and environment from region to region. These abundant differences have been a major factor in creating the curious blend that is Japanese culture as we know it today.

Mt. Fuji at sunset.

Shikoku coastline.

Rice paddies in central Honshu.

Mountains and Oceans

The backbone of this long, scattered line of islands is a slender mountain range stretching down the very middle of the nation. With about 70 percent of the mountains in the range volcanic in origin, this "national divide" falls away at a sharp angle from the mountains to either coast — the Pacific Ocean to the East, and the Sea of Japan to the West. As a result, 31 percent of Japan's land area lies at angles of 20 degrees or more. Change is inescapable with this sort of geographical rarity, as steeply sloped, tree-carpeted mountains and narrow, swift-flowing rivers give way quickly to coastal lowlands.

Returning once again to the LANDSAT picture, we can see patches of yellowish green. These are the basin lands between mountains, and small plains along the coast. They are comparatively low in altitude and flat in their natural lie, and thus suited for human habitation. These regions, however, represent a mere 25 percent of Japan's total land area.

Kaii Higashiyama (1908-), one of modern Japan's most famous painters, has interpreted the natural beauty of Japan not in terms of the limited flats, but rather in the overabundancy of mountainous terrain, surrounded on all sides by ocean waters. Higashiyama describes his vision as follows.

"Mountains and seas — the two primary elements of Japan. As an island nation Japan is surrounded, obviously, on all sides by water, but the coastal regions are anything but uniform.

Haru (spring). This Chinese character combines the symbols for the sun and for new grass sprouts.

Spring: Cherry trees bloom for only a few days. There is a saying in Japanese, "Fall gallantly, like the cherry blossoms."

Following the coast around the nation, one will find quiet, sandy beaches, rough and rugged cliffs, gentle inland seas, turbulent open ocean — countless varieties of natural landscape.

"The Pacific Ocean and the Sea of Japan, two coastlines totally different in character, form the perimeters of Japan, both reaching to small inlets and isles everywhere — in the north, in the south, in the east, in the west. The ice floes of the northern seas in the winter, the sparkling coral reefs in the perennial summer of the southern reaches; Japan is a distant stretch of island land touching different climes and landscapes. A wide range of geographical change, broad variations in the ebb and flow of the seasons, not to mention weather and even time; the oceans of Japan offer us an infinite textbook of natural wonder and beauty.

"Japan's mountains are certainly no less dynamic in their expression of the nation's natural change and variation. This is a nation in which it is impossible to ride in a train or a car for days on end, or to travel through wide, extended plains country. Any flatlands will soon be interrupted by mountain ranges. There are hills and mountains everywhere you go, blanketed in green foliage and covered with frost, fog and clouds, often changing their countenance before one's very eyes. The coming and going of the four seasons is clearly reflected in the mountains of Japan."

While the Japanese people are surrounded on all sides by exquisite natural landscapes, the foundation of their daily lives is anchored in small flatland areas. The industrialization of the post-Meiji Restoration era from about 1868 has increased the importance of the plains. The great majority of the population has moved steadily to the large cities located there, and the natural beauty near these areas continues to be eroded. The mountainous regions which make up most of Japan's land area are progressively becoming depopulated.

There are twice as many Japanese as there are West Germans, British or Italians, and the population density of the nation as a whole in terms of per capita livable land is among the highest in the world.

If all the world's glaciers were to suddenly melt, the plains of Japan would all be submerged as the sea level rose. This means that most of the population would also be inundated as most people live on the coasts, facing the ocean with their backs to the mountains.

Flatlands in northern Honshu.

Ago Bay, Shima Peninsula.

Pearl beds in Ago Bay.

Seto Inland Sea beyond Matsuyama.

The western tip of Shikoku.

The Four Seasons

As so aptly described in words and pictures by Kaii Higashiyama, the clearly defined change of seasons in Japan has made the country's natural environment even more complex and even more subtle in character. On the west extreme of Eurasia in Europe, for example, prevailing westerly winds blow perennially, carrying with them moist, warm air from the ocean's surface. In contrast, on the eastern side, seasonal winds are the norm. In summer, warm, humid winds blow from the Pacific Ocean; while in winter the Siberian cold air masses bring a sustained chill from the north. This is the reason that although both Japan and the U.K. are island nations, Japan has a far more dramatic difference between summer and winter.

Summer in Japan is hot and humid, while the winter cold cuts to the bone. But these extremes are relieved by the seasonal changes, with mild weather in spring and autumn. These four seasons come and go with clockwork regularity.

Japan has no strictly defined rainy season, although varied degrees of precipitation will occur each month of the year. From spring through summer a long wet season drags on, and when the summer heat at last withdraws its muggy clutches, the typhoon season has arrived. Tropical atmospheric depressions generated in the southwest travel a northern route, bending off to the northeast upon approaching Japan. These are known as typhoons, and about four major storms assault Japan annually, bringing strong rains and winds, and often leaving behind great damage and destruction.

In winter, blue skies are customary for Tokyo, Osaka, Kobe and other cities along the Pacific Coast. Crossing over the mountains to the Japan Sea side, however, one is greeted by heavy snowfall. Chilly seasonal winds from Siberia literally inhale ocean water, freezing it into snow which then blankets the coast and immediate inland.

Average precipitation in Japan is about 1,500 millimeters, with certain locales above the 2,000 mm mark. This is over twice the global land area average of 700 mm. The amount of water absorbed by Japan is particularly high when considering that the averages for cities such as London and Paris are only 600 mm.

The LANDSAT image of Japan shows the entire island chain without a single cloud. Such a situation, however, is extremely rare. Japan is continually visited by rain, snow and cloud cover, while fog banks often rise up from the basins and valleys of inland regions. From ancient times, the Japanese have compared the harsh fluctuations and unreliable nature of their nation's weather to the often fickle nature of the human heart.

For centuries the Japanese people have closely observed the cycle of the seasons, gradually developing the wisdom necessary to cope with the changes of each of the four, in order to carry on productive, satisfying lives. One concrete example of such wisdom is the Japanese roof.

The traditional Japanese roof has always been outfitted with openings in the outside walls, which were then overhung with long, low-slung eaves. A common design throughout Asian nations falling in the monsoon zone, these eaves block out the hot sunshine in the summer, but allow the winter sun, which shines at a considerably lower angle, to slip in under their length. And during rains, these long eaves allow dwellers to leave doors open, thereby cooling and brightening the interior. Another Japanese invention is

Natsu (summer). This character conjures up images of a dancer in a summer festival wearing a large mask.

Summer: After the blossoms fall, cherry trees are cloaked with bright new shades of green. Unbaked "cherry rice cakes" are wrapped in these leaves.

Sunrise at Matsushima.

a low wooden veranda placed under the eaves, allowing one to sit down and actually be outside in the midst of nature while still connected to the house itself. In short, the area beneath the roof is a unique space hard to define as either inside or outside, designed to allow the Japanese to become part of the natural world.

Junichiro Tanizaki, the prize-winning Japanese novelist, expressed the Japanese "sense of the roof" in simple, precise terms: "If the Japanese roof is thought of metaphorically as an umbrella, then in Western terms it must coincide with a hat — and a bird-hunting hat at that, with as small a brim as possible to allow direct sunlight to fall close to the edge of the 'eaves.'" At the totally opposite pole is the roof of a modern four-cornered building. While towering high-rises continue to grow within Japan's cities, the Japanese people continue to have difficulty identifying with the roofs (or lack of them) of these structures. Perhaps this is because of the lack of "shadows," a concept which Tanizaki offers as one of the key elements of Japanese esthetics: "Our ancestors, compelled by circumstance to live in dark rooms, gradually discovered the beauty of shadows. And in time, they came to use shadows in their search for natural beauty."

Japan is generally classified as lying in the Temperate Zone, but in fact, while the northern island of Hokkaido is subarctic, the southernmost island groups belong to the subtropics. And seasonal change, a factor so deeply tied to the Japanese consciousness, varies widely in essence and time according to geography.

The diversity of the country's weather can perhaps most graphically be demonstrated by measuring the pattern of the coming of spring to Japan. Japanese traditionally identify the arrival of spring with the blooming of the nation's famous cherry trees. There is much attention paid to the "cherry blossom front," moving steadily from south to north as spring arrives. The southernmost major island of Okinawa is alive with flowers in February, while Tokyo, located in approximately the center of the nation, has its flower-viewing season in late March. This bloom line continues north through April, with the northernmost island of Hokkaido heralding the coming of spring with the trees' pale pink blossoms in May. This extended celebration of spring, then, takes more than 120 days from the southern end to the northern tip of the archipelago.

And this is only a single example of the great concern the Japanese pay to the tones of the different seasons. Northerners are delighted by the initial tidings of spring from the "deep south," and Southerners feel an instinctive need to begin winter preparations when news roundups report the first frost in the north.

There are subtle weather variations even within the same district, and simply traveling from one area to another can bring a change in the weather pattern. The Japanese nation is a complicated weave of weather and land variations, and it is within this pattern that the people of the nation forge their daily modes of existence.

Aki (autumn). The root meaning refers to rice harvesting in the fall.

Japanese Roots

The Japanese island chain has not always been in the configuration photographed so clearly by LANDSAT. Just 200,000 years ago the archipelago was connected in the north to Siberia, and in the south to Korea. Even earlier it was part of the Philippines, Java and other now faraway land masses. And the Sea of Japan was, in prehistoric times, a gigantic lake.

Fossil discoveries dating back to these prehistoric times have revealed that herds of prehistoric elephants once wandered the lands which are now Japan, but eventually died out. The stegodon elephants apparently reached Japan from India, migrating across Burma and China, while mammoths plodded over from the frozen turf of Siberia. Fossilized remains of lions and leopards, which are not found in modern Japan, have also been discovered.

The people of this age apparently were nomadic, moving in search of the animal prey which was their main source of food. The oldest human bones unearthed on the archipelago date back almost 200,000 years.

The question of what route was traveled by the people who eventually became the Japanese race has never really been satisfactorily answered. There are some scholars who theorize that migrating peoples from Indonesia passed through the Philippines, Taiwan and Okinawa. Others give credence to the Indochina-Southern China route or Mongolia-Korean Peninsula route. Weighing all available evidence, the most likely theory is that peoples from the north and the south mingled and interbred, becoming the Japanese race as we know it today.

From that age on, every stage of Japanese history has witnessed assimilation of other peoples from widely scattered regions. There is one theory that the original ancestors of the Japanese Imperial Family — the Yamato Court in the sixth century — can be traced to the Persian highlands. In any event, it is undeniable that Japanese culture is a mix of peoples with originally different lifestyles and customs, who melded together over many centuries.

The true beginnings of a distinctive Japanese culture date back about 10,000 years, to the Jomon period, which lasted until just before the Christian era. This age takes its name from the straw-rope patterns found on the pottery of the period. These patterns were formed by weaving plains grass into rope, which was then pushed and rolled across the wet clay to form the desired design. This type of pottery has only been discovered in Japan.

It was from the middle to the end of the Jomon period, from about 800 to 300 B.C., that the people of the archipelago emerged as a race with distinctive physical characteristics, as homogeneous tribes expanded over most of the island chain. In 1982, archeological diggings yielded wood fragments thought to be from Jomon bathing tubs, drums, and bows, all treated with *urushi* (lacquer). *Urushi* continues to be used widely today on various types of plates and kitchenware, and is valued highly for both its beauty and durability. This Jomon time capsule provides a fascinating link in the long history of Japan.

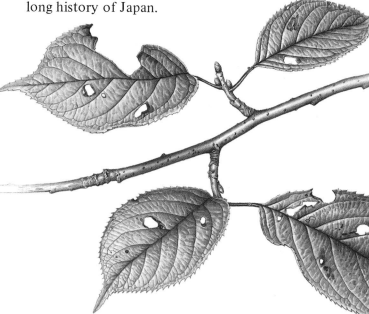

Fishing boats at a port in Okinawa.

Mountains overlooking Otaru City.

A river running through Kanazawa City, Honshu.

A lumber operation in the Kiso mountains.

From the Soil

Agriculture has had a major influence on the Japanese personality and culture. This is especially true of rice-paddy farming, which is still practiced on 40 percent of Japan's total arable land. Summers in Japan are tropical, with hot, muggy weather the rule, and the largely alluvial soil-based plains lend themselves to irrigation. As a result, rice farming naturally became the core of the country's agriculture.

Paddy farming techniques appear to have

Autumn: Yellow cherry tree leaves scatter as the shades of autumn deepen. For Japanese, it is a time of reflection.

Irises at Meiji Shrine, Tokyo.

Maples at Nisonin Temple, Kyoto.

come from China in the third century B.C., and their arrival signaled the end of the Jomon age. The methodology entered Japan through northern Kyushu, where Japanese culture first took recognizable roots. This focus gradually shifted to the Kinki district, and the Nara plain, location of the ancient Yamato Imperial Court, which had the highest rice yield per unit of area in Japan until the early 20th century.

Despite the high level of today's technology, rice growing is still dependent on the weather. If rainfall is extremely low during the wet season, the Japanese will grow concerned about the rice harvest in the fall. Cool summers also trigger worries about whether that year's crop will be a good one or not.

It is difficult to combat weather with only human resources. In ancient times when rice cultivation was almost entirely dependent on the whims of nature, weather determined the nation's fate. People came to accept natural disasters as acts of the gods beyond human control, and struggled to dwell in harmony with natural forces. Such an approach is far removed from the experiences of other peoples — such as the northern Europeans who struggled with the power of the ocean; or the western-bound pioneers of 19th century America, who fought against the harsh weather of the Great Plains just to stay alive. Rather than opposing nature, the Japanese learned to adapt their daily lives to devastating forces which they could not control.

Arising from this came a religiosity which tended to perceive "God" in all aspects of nature. Gods were thought to be present in the stars, vegetation and soil. There was even an official god in charge of the toilet. It was said that the eight million gods of Japan would congregate each October in Izumo in the Sanin district, and the tenth lunar month of the traditional Japanese calendar was known as *kannazuki,* literally, "the month all the gods are away."

Although Japan is generally counted as a Buddhist nation, of the current population of just under 120 million, believers in Buddhism are said to number 83,600,000 persons, while devotees of Shinto are 81,100,000. This is because neither Buddhism nor Shinto is considered the faith of a single god, and as a result few Japanese really consider themselves exclusively "Buddhist." Although Buddhism arrived

Winter: Snow accumulates on the bare cherry branches. Beneath this white blanket is a sense of the spring to come.

from China in the sixth century A.D., the Buddhist idea of transmigration of souls was perfectly matched to the deeply-rooted perception of nature held by the Japanese people. The Buddhist concept that the evils of a past life were the inevitable cause for the woes of the present one, which then again would provide key connections to the next life, was perfectly compatible with existing animist religions. Throughout all and despite — or possibly because of — this philosophy, the Japanese entrusted all to nature, and accepted their situation passively.

To this day Japanese will press their hands together in prayer at a Buddhist temple, then proceed next door to a Shinto shrine to clap hands in the traditional prayer of that religion. And there are still many elderly Japanese who bow their heads in respectful silence whenever passing the small shrines often found in suburban and country neighborhoods. It is clear that there is still no one particular "God" in Japan.

Religion in Japan could very well be defined as "nature worship." *Amaterasu-omikami,* the key deity worshipped at Ise Shrine, the mecca of Shinto, is the sun goddess. Naturally the most important single element of nature is the sun, and the Japanese often refer to the source of our light and heat in honorific terms — *ohisama.* The "moods" of the sun hold tremendous sway over the success or failure of paddy farming, and so it was literally impossible to worship it to excess.

Rice cultivation requires strict planning, with planting and harvesting timed and great care taken between these periods to ensure the health of the crop. Besides timing, group labor is also a major factor in growing good rice. Recent advances have made it possible for many farm chores to be handled by machines, but in the past such tasks were carried out by informal neighborhood cooperatives, with the key to swift completion being mutual support and familiarity with the work itself. Whether the existence of cooperative groups led the Japanese to grow rice with such care, or rice growing created Japan's cooperative group ethic can be argued. But there is no doubt that the same ethic is still dramatically apparent in today's industrialized society in the form of close teamwork in plants and offices.

Careful attention to one's tools was another natural by-product of this work ethic. In Japan, the origins of material culture lie in the tools used for harvesting. The wide variety of such tools perfected in ancient times changed very little through the middle to modern ages. People experienced nature with their five senses, and through the use of hoes and ploughs perceived the inner workings of the natural world and entered into meaningful communication with the larger forces around them. Subsequent improvements in technique were viewed as a way to improve the quality of this indispensable communication.

One pinnacle of material culture in Japan was the traditional Japanese sword. The highly skilled swordsmiths who carried on this proud tradition through Japan's feudal ages were forced to alter their livelihoods when ordered to relinquish this trade at the time of the Meiji Restoration. The great majority moved into other fields — such as forging farm tools and home implements, from swords to ploughshares. And so, without any hesitation, these artisans returned to direct contact with the land.

Overshadowed by the overpowering strength of the natural world, they have pondered their own hands and tools, diligently applying themselves to finding ways to make each harvest more fruitful than its predecessor.

With no belief in a single absolute deity, the Japanese developed no concept of any all-powerful, transcendent being. Their mental energies were directed instead toward a sustained search for beauty within the realm of everyday life. This inward-directedness formed the cornerstone for today's Japanese culture.

Kyoto cuisine: (clockwise from above left) confectionaries and their molds, eggplant pickles, rice cakes and a light lunch.

Living with Wood

Agricultural implements were the spearhead of tool development in Japan. Helping progress in this area was the relative abundance of trees, whose wood was used to produce farm tools of all kinds.

Generous rainfall over the entire nation gave birth to lush forests. The growing season for vegetation in almost all regions ranges from 200 to 365 days, and with the climate stretching

Fuyu (winter). An expression of the freezing cold air of this season.

from subarctic to subtropic extremes there is a tremendous variety of plant life — over 4,000 kinds of seed plants alone. This is a volume actually on a par with that of the vast geographical block of North America. There are also many different types of forests, including subtropical tree varieties, evergreen broad-leafed trees in the warmer regions, deciduous broad-leafed trees in the cooler regions and evergreen coniferous trees in the subarctic zones.

Wooden buildings are an apt reflection of Japan's climate and geography, and wood is well suited to the aesthetic senses of the nation's people, who maintain a reverence for the finer details of everyday life. The architecture of ancient Japan was virtually devoid of stone structures, and even if such buildings had been erected they would most likely have failed to weather the long journey over the centuries. In the hot and humid summer of Japan, for example, stone would have been plagued by dew condensation, making such structures uncom-

fortable to live in and short-lived.

Another factor working against the use of stone as a building material is the frequency of earthquakes in Japan. Of all earthquakes in the world, 10 percent occur in the Japanese islands. An old proverb names the four most frightening things in Japan as earthquakes, thunder, fires and fathers — the fact that earthquakes rate first mention in this list is an indication of the deep fear harbored by the Japanese of this particular type of natural disaster. Stone and brick structures are not designed to stand up under heavy seismic attack, and the rubble that remains after such a building crumbles is not only useless but also extremely difficult to clean up. A wood structure, on the other hand, can be rebuilt even if it has completely collapsed.

Street fortune-teller.

Yuzen Kimono.

Approach to Nisonin Temple, Kyoto.

Japanese architecture has been forced to adapt to harsh natural forces such as earthquakes and typhoons. One particularly effective method of building devised centuries ago is the use of "pin joints" in buildings. Deep notches are cut into connecting pillars to eliminate the need for nails, and this allows buildings to shake and shift in the throes of an earthquake, softening the vibration and stress on individual structural members to lessen the chance of collapse. The ability of five-storied pagodas to survive earthquake after earthquake over the years is due to this pin-joint construction. The "pliable construction" of high-rise buildings perfected by modern Japanese architects to minimize earthquake hazards is an advance ranking alongside the pin-joint method — both major breakthroughs in their respective historical periods.

Japan's oldest existing structure is Horyu-ji, a huge temple in Nara built in 607, and reconstructed in 712 after destruction by fire. There are many other shrines and temples around the nation which have withstood all elements for well over a millenium. Such cultural treasures have received generous protection over the centuries, including rigorous upkeep and frequent restoration efforts. Tsunekazu Nishioka (1908-), a carpenter specializing in shrine and temple construction who now oversees Horyu-ji, offers the following comments about the importance of wood in Japanese culture:

"Japan has always been a nation blessed with great forests, and anywhere you go you find an abundant supply of large trees. The ancient Japanese were awed by the ability of such trees to stand up against storms, earthquakes and other disasters, and learned much from observing them. You could almost say that many Japanese have been raised by trees.

"I have a great respect for our ancestors, who studied trees and then applied this knowledge to perfect sophisticated architectural techniques, many of which are still in use today. It is a real marvel that wooden structures built over ten centuries ago still exist. And this is what motivates me most deeply in my work — those of us living today must realize our responsibilities to future generations by preserving this wonderful, uniquely Japanese architectural tradition."

Ayu dinner.

A typical market.

Festivals have always been an important part of the Japanese cultural calendar.

The special characteristics of wood have also been skillfully and intricately applied to the construction of homes. There are thousands of houses extant which were originally built between the 12th and 19th centuries. All of these homes were built with local materials and the differing characteristics of each material have been carefully emphasized. The structures of such houses provide a showcase for the inherent natural beauty of wood, with detail and lines openly displayed. The majority of such homes have exposed frames visible all the way to the ceiling, hefty pillars and curved pieces of polished wood integrated into the walls and supports, along with other picturesque touches.

The use of pin joints was not limited to temples, but applied to private homes as well. And if wood is considered the "skeleton" of such a house, then earth, reeds, paper and other materials formed the "flesh." Thick, earth-packed walls were effective in absorbing humidity — a definite plus for comfort and health. Thatched roofs, sometimes over a meter thick, were an ingenious means to guard the interior against overheating. Another touch was planting trees near the house, placing them strategically to block the heat of the afternoon sun and to soften the force of strong winds.

Traditional Japanese houses differ greatly from their counterparts in the West. For example, few rooms are categorized by function, and there are no "living rooms" or "guest rooms" as such.

Homes were often expected to last several hundred years, so great efforts were made at the design stage to allow sufficient latitude for accommodating wide shifts in family makeups and lifestyles. With rooms divided only by sliding doors made of paper or other lightweight materials, living spaces of different sizes and shapes could be created as the need arose. Wooden structures also lent themselves to easy alteration or addition of new rooms and wings.

The danger of fire taught dwellers to set aside one corner of the site as a storage area for valuables — with both ceiling and walls formed into frameworks about 30 centimeters thick and packed with mud and plaster. Other than the doors, contact with the outside world was limited to small windows, designed primarily to admit light. The interior was well sealed, with the thick walls maintaining steady temperature and humidity levels. Even when a fire would rage in the immediate vicinity, the valuables inside would remain unscathed if the windows and door were closed. During the air raids of World War II when whole districts would be burned to the ground, many of these mud-packed depositories and their contents were found to have survived completely intact.

Private dwelling in central Honshu.

Home in northern Honshu.

Today, as modern architectural designs from Europe and America are gaining increased popularity, and high-rise apartment buildings are steadily transforming the face and fiber of Japanese cities, there are still many people who want to live in homes built of wood using traditional architectural techniques, despite the fact Japan now relies upon imports for the majority of its wood for homes and other purposes.

Yoshio Akioka (1922-), a professor at Kyoritsu Women's University and an industrial designer who has made a thorough study of carpentry tools in Japan, has this to say about wooden homes:

"One of the best things about living in a natural wood house is during the humid rainy season the wood will absorb the moisture in the air. Then in cold winter weather the same wood will emit moisture — it is a natural form of air conditioning which is good for the health. So even after it has been felled a tree continues to live and breathe in a new form."

Despite the heavy reliance on imports for its wood needs Japan and its people continue to carry on a deep love affair with this finest and most versatile of natural materials.

Washing newly dyed Kimono.

A Kyoto temple in the woods.

Natural Traditions

There is an old saying in Japan that "In the sky there are the seasons; on the earth there is the essence; in materials there is beauty; and in work there is craftsmanship." In other words, in the quest to produce a beautiful, superior product, the natural elements — seasons and weather, earth and environment, and good raw materials — must be present, and then blended together with consummate skill.

The Japanese place great value on the quality of their everyday lives, and their aesthetics reflect this. The culture casts great respect on those designated as craftsmen and artisans, whose skills involve the power to become one with the surrounding natural environment and the ability to create objects of art which reflect this spiritual harmony.

The Japanese have come to believe that since nature is beautiful, things which receive the blessings of nature must also be beautiful. The beauty of traditional arts has been carried through to the present day, and some of the modern masters of the traditional can be found in Chapter II. One of these "living national treasures," the fourteenth generation master ceramics artisan Kakiemon Sakaida (1934 -),

A Japanese Garden.

spends three months each year roaming fields to observe flowers in their natural setting.

"I always carry my sketchbook with me on my roamings, but I never consider transferring the sketches of the flowers that I see as-is to my porcelain ware. I would have to represent the flower so it would fit on the dish, and as a result its true strength and life would die. When I truly draw a flower as it is, the knowledge of every aspect of that flower becomes part of me. When that happens I no longer need my sketches to create my design. My father (the thirteenth generation artisan, who died in 1982) used to tell me that my sketches looked too much like my designs. I believe now I finally understand what he meant."

Kakiemon believes that the genuine strength of nature being borrowed for his ceramic art is not fully embodied in cut flowers. There is, however, another cultural application which *does* use cut flowers — *ikebana,* or flower arrangement. Unfortunately, the truly subtle nuances of the Japanese word *ikebana* cannot be communicated by the English rendition of "flower arrangement." In Japanese, the word connotes putting "vigor" or "life" into flowers — in other words, taking a cut flower which would simply wither away and die if abandoned in the field, and adding the magic of the artist to give it new life and form.

The Japanese have always had great attachment to nature, and perhaps it was the attempt to adapt to the subtle structure of the natural world that propelled artists and artisans to develop the detailed techniques that are their trademark today.

Nevertheless, since the Meiji Restoration Japan's rapid industrialization has eradicated much of the natural beauty in certain areas. Agriculture, once the very cornerstone of Japan's technology, now supplies a mere 36 percent of the food necessary to feed the nation. Nature, long regarded by the Japanese as the soul of their lives and thoughts, has begun to decay from the bottom up. Consequently, the problem of how to preserve the beauty and force of the natural world, while continuing to sustain vital technological development, is undoubtedly the single most important issue now being faced by today's Japan.

A carefully manicured garden.

Edo period teahouse.

Water basin in a Japanese garden.

Carp in a canal.

Meisho Temple, Kyoto.

Old warehouse.

Closeup of a traditional warehouse.

Cultural Inheritances

The continuing undertone of the modernization of Japan from the Meiji Restoration on has been the overwhelming influx of Western influences. Nearly overnight, it seemed, Japan was transformed from an agricultural to an industrialized nation.

Werner Mayer-Larsen of *Der Spiegel,* one of West Germany's leading weekly magazines, once made the observation that "Japan entered the ranks of industrially developed nations without ever spending time as a developing nation. It never accepted large groups of skilled immigrants from developed nations; nor did large volumes of foreign capital pour in to support its development. Yet it has grown, all on its own, to become one of the world's foremost industrial powers."

One major reason for this success is that Japan was never conquered or occupied by another nation. Throughout its history, in fact, there are few if any examples of the Japanese being assaulted by external military forces. Perhaps this clean record is the direct result of being an island nation lying in relative isolation at the far eastern reaches of Asia.

The absence of outside military interference dulled any real desire to rebuff foreign cultures. The Japanese have even been called a "highly curious, superficial race," and whether or not the latter adjective is accurate, it certainly is a fact that they are a people who have always moved forward spontaneously and vigorously to absorb cultural influences of all kinds and from all quarters. These new influences were then mixed with their own culture, and either assimilated or allowed to co-exist.

The writing of the Japanese language is an excellent example. The first step in creating written Japanese involved borrowing *kanji* (ideographic characters) from the Chinese. The second phase was the simplification or abbreviation of *kanji,* on which was based the invention of the *kana* syllabaries used to represent the sounds of Japanese phonetically. Modern written Japanese is a combination of *kanji* and *kana,* and there is an excellent chance that many of the sounds used in ancient times have survived as-is over the centuries.

Ever since the Meiji Restoration the Japanese have been very open to Western languages and on paper these foreign words are written in one of the *kana* alphabets — *katakana.* The result? A written language resplendent with foreign words, ideas and expressions.

The past century, during which the economic foundation of the nation has shifted from farming to industrialization, was an age in which the Japanese tradition of active borrowing from overseas sources clearly surfaced. A list of examples of assimilation of things foreign — on both the micro and macro levels — would fill many volumes.

One particularly interesting example is *anpan,* a bread roll filled with bean jam, which made its debut in the Meiji era. Bread, an introduction from the West, was filled with a type of sweet bean paste which has been a favorite of the Japanese for centuries — a true blend of East and West. It is said that a Western-style confectionery in the Ginza district of Tokyo run by two brothers invented this unique delicacy. One brother studied the latest advances in bread-baking in Yokohama, then the nation's foremost port where many foreigners came to do business and live, while the other brother studied traditional Japanese-style confections in Tokyo. Then, as this success story goes, the two brothers joined forces to develop a new food which took Japan by storm and has never lost its deep-rooted popularity.

Long before the Meiji Restoration, in 1543, a single tip of Western technology truly startled Japan — a musket-type rifle carried to a southern island of Japan by Portuguese sailors. To the Japanese, whose primary weapons at that time were the bow and sword, this was a revolutionary discovery. Yet in a mere year's time, and solely on the basis of observation and imitation, swordsmiths had produced Japan's first rifle. A quick glance at examples of this ancient domestic version shows little if any difference between it and the Portuguese prototype, but a more detailed examination reveals a subtle divergence — a distinctive curved stock design.

This stock is reminiscent of the gentle warp of the traditional Japanese sword. The predecessor of this weapon was a straight sword brought over from China. The Japanese added the distinctive curve that defined a new concept in swords.

This is just one example of a traditional trait which continues to deeply color the behavior and philosophy of the Japanese today: technology and ideas adopted from overseas sources are enhanced by the fine techniques and craftsmanship cultivated by Japanese artisans for decades, sometimes centuries, and perfected to yet higher realms of excellence.

While craftsmanship is often said to be a deterrent to high productivity in today's highly industrialized world, in Japan such technical excellence has produced just the opposite results — healthy economic growth and solid advances in social infrastructure and lifestyles. These are the benefits of a cultural background emphasizing cooperation with both people and nature — highly effective group behavior perfected by Japanese communities from the days when the nation was predominantly rural combined with an enduring commitment to harmonious adaptation to the natural world.

It is common knowledge nowadays that while Japan is a nation rich in natural splendor, it is also an island nation which relies on imports for 99 percent of its mineral resources. To close the gap with other regions in terms of technology, major emphasis was placed on education in the Meiji era. From that time on and even more so now, learning was a foremost priority for all levels of Japanese society. Modern industrial education and training has been carefully underpinned by the traditional demand for and respect of craftmanship. The skilled master tradesmen who emerged from this process provided the initial push in Japan's headlong dash toward industrialization.

There is one serious problem, however. Although in strict economic terms Japan now stands at the front ranks of the developed nations of the world, there is a vital need to ponder the immediate future. What original and meaningful contributions can Japan make to the world community in the years and decades ahead? The tradition of craftsmanship formulated by absorption of, coexistence with and assimilation of the most desired elements of foreign culture, now finds itself at a confusing and vitally important crossroads at which key decisions must be made about new directions for the future.

If the LANDSAT satellite were able to zoom in close enough to the earth's surface, its pass over the expansive, chaotic Japanese capital of Tokyo would show a group of skyscrapers clustered at the west side of the metropolis — the city's Shinjuku subcenter.

The tallest member of this select group is the Shinjuku Center Building, towering 216 meters and 54 floors above the ground. And equally impressive is the 22,400 square-meter site upon which the structure stands, which has been planted with approximately 44,000 trees in 30 different varieties in a careful attempt to trace the progression of the seasons in the city.

Next door is the Shinjuku Nomura Building, 203 meters high with 50 stories above ground. In the thick vegetation surrounding it, bird feeders have been strategically placed, and they are kept full of seed by a maintenance company. In the midst of this man-made subcity a small bird sanctuary has been allowed to prosper.

Kanazawa City, the "Little Kyoto" of the Hokuriku district.

Old warehouses along a Kurashiki City street.

Five-story pagoda in Asakusa, Tokyo.

The past is still alive in Japan's cities.

Bullet train crossing over an expressway.

Skyscrapers are now a familiar cityscape.

If LANDSAT then swung its eye to the dense housing area surrounding these skyscrapers, another intricate pattern would appear on its tracking screen: in a maze of tiny twisting streets and alleys, hundreds of small potted plants rest on the patches of space available before cramped entryways, or on amazingly narrow second-story verandas. Miniature gardens and tiny root-tied bonsai trees have been a part of the Japanese people's living space for centuries. And in small home gardens you will find scaled-down mountains, valleys and waterfalls sculpted into the available land in a time-honored attempt to recreate a tiny patch of Japan's natural wonders in a backyard.

The desire for more comfort, beauty and quality within limited space has not been dulled by the rapid urbanization in Japan's cities — if anything, it has been given even more vigorous inspiration. The aesthetic tradition of the Japanese has been, and continues to be, a drive to mold one's immediate surroundings into a private, exclusive universe, which will provide maximum enjoyment and peace of mind. The master craftsmen who have learned to always reflect the finest details of Japanese culture in their artistry, have paid close mind to the conditions and feelings of their countrymen, and have perfected the art of responding to the desires of the ordinary man with sympathy and understanding.

Let us turn next to the Japanese masters who have carried on traditional arts to the present day. We have traveled to their homes, their studios, listened to their thoughts. It is our sincere hope that they, through their words, ideas and art, can offer the world new insights into Japan and possibly even new ways of existing in this era of accelerating change.

Travel with us then, through the following pages as we trace the sources of Japanese tradition, of Japanese harmony, of Japanese quality.

Main street of Ginza, Tokyo.

Traditions and Technology

In Japan there are "Living National Treasures"—men and women with skills so fine and rare that they are officially recognized as part of the nation's cultural heritage.

These artists and craftsmen and their forebears are the models for Japan's current excellence in things technological. The quality of their work and their dedication to perfection have few equals anywhere in the world.

In our second chapter, we will visit different parts of Japan to take a close look at the skills and ideas of these "treasures" and other masters of the traditional arts.

BUILDING

TATERU
"To Build"

Master carpenter Nishioka measuring *hinoki*.

The Temple Carpenter and the Pagoda

The world's oldest wooden structures are located in Nara, in the Kinki district of Japan, at the ancient location of the Yamato Court — the distant ancestors of today's Imperial Family. These are found at Horyu-ji, a huge temple complex in the south section of Nara City which is said to have burned to the ground in the latter half of the seventh century, only to be rebuilt early in the next century. In the 1,200 years since, this temple has been carefully maintained by a long line of master carpenters, who have seen to all necessary upkeep and repairs.

Tsunekazu Nishioka (1908-) was born into one of the families which has traditionally handled this task. He has literally dedicated his life to Horyu-ji and other ancient temples in the Nara area, and is considered *the* authority in the field of temple and pagoda architecture.

Major repairs to Horyu-ji were started in 1934, and while interrupted during World War II, lasted for 20 years. Nishioka at the age of only 26 was put in charge of repairing the Toinrai-do, the temple's east pavilion, and fulfilled this task admirably. The master recalls those days:

"I was stunned by the tremendous longevity of the white cedar used in the structure. The pillars were over a thousand years old, and although they were slightly darkened and decayed on the outside, when they were planed down two or three millimeters they gave off a sweet, fresh fragrance like new-cut wood.

"The supporting beams were huge log lengths, which were bent and sagging under the weight of the massive roof. However, about two or three days after we removed the tile and earth insulation from the roof, we were amazed to find that the beams seemed to regain their original form. The white cedar had continued to live through the centuries, and we stood in awe of its strength."

In Japanese this white cedar tree is called *hinoki* — a coniferous evergreen native to Japan which from ancient times has provided the wood most widely used for buildings, Buddhist sculptures and other works meant to endure.

Hinoki is extremely durable. The research of Jiro Kohara, Ph.D., Professor of Chiba Institute of Technology, has revealed that *hinoki* maintains its original strength even after a thousand years, and that the wood used in Horyu-ji has changed very little from the time the temple complex was originally consecrated. Kohara compared the *hinoki* with *keyaki* (zelkova), a representative broad-leafed tree native to Japan and noted for its fine, hard wood. He found that while the *keyaki* wood is twice as hard as *hinoki* when it is first cut, it ages much more rapidly. After 100 years it had deteriorated more than *hinoki* will after 500 years.

Often called "the last temple carpenter," Nishioka's greatest concern is that there will be no one to carry on his traditional techniques.

Hinoki also maintains its rich, fragrant odor and the pale cherry-blossom hue of its wood, bringing deep sensual satisfaction to the Japanese people, whose love of plain, unfinished woodwork has always made them loath to paint over natural wood surfaces.

However, Japan's forest resources are rapidly being depleted. In more recent years Tsunekazu Nishioka has been involved in the reconstruction of Yakushi-ji, another famous Nara temple, for which huge amounts of *hinoki* have been needed. In the west pagoda of the complex alone, a three-storied structure 34.1 meters high, about 300 *hinoki* trees one thousand years old were used. So many trees could not be procured within Japan alone, and a significant amount of Taiwanese *hinoki* wood was imported to fill the need.

There is one entry in Nishioka's personal history which catches the eye. The master carpenter attended an agricultural school in his teens — a slightly strange credential for a journeyman carpenter. In fact, however, he was sent to this school by his grandfather, who himself served as the head carpenter of the Horyu-ji. Nishioka describes his grandfather's philosophy behind this act:

"Man was born from the soil, and to the soil he will return. Trees are also cultivated in the soil, and someday will return to the soil. Buildings are constructed upon soil. Without soil, there would be no people, there would be no trees, there would be no temples. It is impossible to be a great carpenter without realizing the sanctity of the soil."

This thinking follows the drift of an ancient Japanese proverb: "When buying wood, look to the mountain, not to the trees." In other words, trees grow in infinite variety, depending on the terrain, exposure to the sun and many other factors. Like human beings, each tree has a

The Yakushi-ji West Pagoda, one of Nishioka's greatest works.

Rough planing tools like these have been used for hundreds of years.

The master at his drawing board.

The pin joints at one corner of the Yakushi-ji Pagoda.

Close-up of pin joints.

An ancient manuscript detailing the fundamentals of pagoda building and related carpentry techniques.

The *yariganna* (spear plane) is one of the tools temple carpenters consider an "extension of the hands."

different personality. Therefore, when buying trees, first understand the personality of the mountain which has nurtured the trees, and then buy up this entire mountain. Creating buildings which bring to life the personalities of trees raised in nature is something Japanese inherit from their ancestors. Nishioka continues:

"To grasp the personality of a tree, you must converse with that tree. Whenever I fell a tree, before I raise the saw I pray, 'I pledge, as a temple carpenter, that I will do nothing which will extinguish the life of this tree.' "

The core of Japanese wooden architecture is the framework. The building materials are carefully cut, with notches carved into each part to be connected into the supporting frame. Most components are assembled in this way. Pagoda architecture shows this technique developed to the highest degree of excellence. Intricate combinations of minutely detailed components rise up into exquisite pagoda towers. Nishioka mentioned the West Pagoda of the Yakushi-ji Temple, whose reconstruction team he headed, as an excellent example. Each story of the three-tiered tower has four corners, with each of these corners containing about 40 separate components. The pagoda in its entirety might be compared to an extremely complex three-dimensional jigsaw puzzle.

One of the most impressive accomplishments of temple carpenters is their ability to skillfully blend the separate elements of individual trees into their architecture. Every tree is shaped uniquely by nature, being twisted to the right, to the left, then back to the right again by a wide range of environmental factors. The master carpenters of ancient Japan learned to follow the lines of the wood, until the ultimate balance of these right- and left-running forces comes out at "zero."

The carpenters of Horyu-ji have handed down the following philosophy over the centuries, which is regarded as a true doctrine of the trade.

"To form a pagoda is to form wood.

To form wood is to form the tree.

To form the tree is to form a man.

To form a man is to form the mind.

To form the mind is to understand the craftsman.

The master craftsman who errs is unworthy of his trade."

This saying speaks of awakening to the knowledge that the formation of wood for building a pagoda is nothing other than the formation of the mind, and that, only when all carpenters unite their minds in this spirit of understanding, can a truly excellent structure be completed.

While his grandfather was still alive and in good health, Nishioka's family owned a certain hilly area covered with oak trees. But this was not a forest from which wood was procured for building — the trees were used for forming the stocks of planes which would be used in the carpentry itself. The planes used by his grandfather, his father, by Nishioka himself and his colleagues were all made from trees in this forest, and all were cut and designed by the person destined to use them. Thus, the tools used for sophisticated craftsmanship are also grown from the earth's soil.

During the restoration of the Kondo, the main pavilion of Horyu-ji, Nishioka produced a *yariganna* (spear plane) as a sort of experiment. Apparently a type of double-edged blade attached to an extended pole, this tool is thought to have been a well-guarded secret of the excellence of traditional Japanese carpentry. While cut marks believed made by this particular tool are still visible on the beams of Horyu-ji, by the beginning of the Edo period (1615-1868) it had just about grown obsolete. Its specific use appears to have been as a finishing tool for the more intricate parts of a temple. Nishioka, therefore, re-created the tool relying solely on his imagination. He speaks of the attachment ancient craftsmen felt toward their tools, based on his own experience in re-creating the *yariganna*:

"*Hinoki* wood cut with a *yariganna* is immaculately smooth to the touch, and rain drops bounce off cleanly upon contact. I feel this to be one of the reasons that ancient wooden structures survive longer than those erected in modern times. The electric planes available today make work go faster, but the surfaces they produce are rough and uneven, and since rainwater is not cleanly repelled the decaying process is accelerated."

Nishioka longs for the excellence of the past, when the craftsman was conjoined with his materials and tools in an exquisitely creative unity of purpose. He is particularly fond of standing beside the pagoda which he restored with his own hands, using methods developed in ancient times. When in the midst of a powerful silence the thick central beam running down the middle of the structure creaks — a sound like splitting to a layman's ears — Nishioka hears "the voices of the trees answering me." This is not the sound of a beam which has begun to rend and will soon collapse; rather, it is the voice of a tree celebrating its new existence, its new life, as the heart of something beautiful.

It is often said in Japan that trees have two lives. A tree that has already lived 1,000 years may very well live for another millenium after it has been cut down, in the form of a wooden building. For this reason, Tsunekazu Nishioka, who has been called the last traditional temple carpenter involved in extensive planning and design, feels uneasy about the future. "I wonder" he says, "if the pagoda I have constructed will survive for 1,000 years, like those built in ancient times."

Nishioka is now involved in restoring the central gate of Yakushi-ji. Dressed in an indigo-dyed *hanten* livery coat with a white towel tied around his head, he is the epitome of the traditional Japanese carpenter. Yet on top of his work desk, beside numerous unfurled blueprints, is one of the newest tools of carpentry. Gone are the old measuring sticks and string of the past. In their place is a sparkling, beeping computer.

The master's black and red ink pads.
He has used them both for over 30 years
in marking the wood he will sculpt.

Shintaro Okubo accepts the challenge of creating a miniature pagoda.

His second challenge is to make a 13-story pagoda.

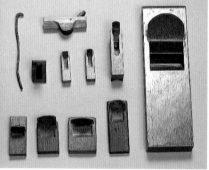

A miniature structure calls for miniature planes (a normal plane is at the right).

The curved plane used to give roofs their distinctive "warp."

A House Carpenter Lives Out a Dream

An old Japanese proverb says that, "Even the smallest insect has a large soul." It expresses well the way in which Shintaro Okubo (1905-), an elderly yet relatively unknown carpenter feels pride in his work. Okubo followed in his father's footsteps and began building ordinary houses. From early in life he was envious of temple carpenters, who were contracted by Buddhist temples and Shinto shrines to design and build or restore magnificent pagodas and pavilions. Ever since becoming a carpenter, Okubo thought that at least once in his life he would like to try his hand at erecting a pagoda.

Then, in the autumn of his lifetime, this "small insect" fulfilled his lifelong wish.

In one of the most exclusive neighborhoods in central Tokyo, the Takanawa district of Minato Ward, amidst a cluster of high-rise buildings runs a street of old houses and stores retaining the antiquity and flavor of the Edo period. In the inner depths of this winding alley, surrounded by temporary construction shacks, a five-story pagoda rises 3.8 meters into the air. Built using the very same techniques as Japan's most famous pagodas, this miniature is the fruition of Okubo's long-cherished dream.

In the postwar era Okubo spent the hours he wasn't building houses collecting *hinoki.* This was the beginning of his plan to build a pagoda that would hold its own against its ancient predecessors, and more importantly, satisfy Okubo himself.

He launched this project at age 65, when most Japanese men would be long since retired from the workaday world. Not Okubo, though. He turned to the dream that had long burned deep within his soul.

Okubo traveled to Nara and Kyoto to view Japan's oldest and most famous pagodas. But as he was only an ordinary tourist, he was unable to take careful measurements, or observe the delicate interior construction. Rather, he had to content himself with visual measurements made by holding his hands up to judge distances. According to Okubo, the technology of the carpenter does not vary. "The size of the rafters which reach from the support pillars to the eaves is the standard which in turn determines the size of all other parts," he notes, referring to the knowledge that Japanese pagodas are in actuality elaborately designed mosaics.

Okubo used a six-mat room in his home as a design studio and workshop. He ran into problems, however, with erecting the central pillar for his 3.8 meter pagoda. The method used for pagoda construction is to build up this central pillar, which stands like a tree trunk running up through the middle of the structure, with the separate stories then added to this framework, from the ground level up. A pillar as high as the one Okubo had in mind, however, could never fit into his Japanese-style house with its traditionally low ceiling. To solve this problem, Okubo decided that he would build up the central pillar gradually in sections, linked to each story as it was completed.

This may very well be the same method used in ancient times to erect the five-story pagoda at Horyu-ji temple in Nara, said to be the most beautiful of all Japanese pagodas. The central pillar of this full-scale pagoda consists of two separate lengths of timber connected together.

"As I began to cut and shape my building materials, my sense of the elaborate beauty of traditional wooden architecture was renewed once again. This was a sensation absent in the old stone or brick buildings."

The construction of Okubo's pagoda required eight years, and was completed when he was 73. He mentioned that there are a few other carpenters who have organized similar miniature pagoda projects. He says modestly: "Anyone who understands the spirit of carpentry and is patient and willing to study a bit can accomplish the same thing." This humility is impressive, because Okubo's range of expertise now ranges from pagoda-building, said to be the true essence of wooden architecture, all the way down to construction of normal houses. So, inhabiting the foothills nestled beneath the peaks of technological excellence of the masters, are numerous lesser-known "small insects," working in the same time-honored traditions.

But Okubo is not yet satisfied. Having tested his abilities, he is now determined to do something never done before.

He considers the 13-story pagoda of Danzan Shrine in Nara "the condensation of all Japanese architecture," and has already begun work on a one-eighth scale miniature of the structure.

A true craftsman remains a craftsman, as long as he breathes.

Hinoki, the wood there never is enough of.

Okubo carefully dusts his pagoda every morning.

Skyscrapers in the new Shinjuku "downtown."

High-Rises in Earthquake Country

On September 1, 1923 a major earthquake centered on Tokyo rocked the entire southern Kanto region. Measured at magnitude 7.9 on the Japanese seismic scale, this quake was one of the greatest ever to hit Japan, where this particular brand of natural disaster is a common occurrence. It left over 100,000 persons either killed or missing, and 580,000 houses totally destroyed. Eight and nine-story structures, considered to be the most modern buildings in Japan at the time, collapsed. But not the 32.3 meter-high, five-story wooden pagoda at Kanei-ji Temple in Ueno Park.

There are many pagodas in Japan which have survived the rains, winds and snows of 1,000 years or more in good stead — along with earthquakes. There is a saying that "a pagoda may fall under the force of a storm, but will withstand an earthquake."

There was one man who took an especially active interest in this phenomenon. He is

Kiyoshi Muto (1903-), currently director of the Muto Institute of Structural Mechanics. He was a student in architecture at Tokyo University in 1923.

Not until after World War II did the Japanese begin research into the relationship between architecture and earthquakes. In America, meanwhile, a project started during the war to develop a device capable of measuring the shocks of unusually strong earthquakes. Professor Muto, who was teaching at his own alma mater at the time, launched his own major project in the field.

To Muto, who began his career as a scholar studying aseismic construction, the wonder of the five-story pagoda was difficult to put aside. He built model after model and subjected them to a wide range of scientific experiments. The results confirmed that the tenacity of the pagoda design was due to the intricate intermingling of wood components. When assaulted by strong vibrations the individual parts would sway and rub together, alleviating the force of the shocks, so that vibrations were kept below a fixed level. Muto's detailed tests proved that as long as the ground surface under a pagoda did not pitch and roll in excess of 70 centimeters, the structure would not collapse. Earthquakes this strong rarely if ever occur, which is almost undeniable proof that pagodas will never be downed by such seismic catastrophes.

Professor Muto was later to become the pioneer of "earthquake-proof" high-rise building design. The concept that dramatically opened the door to skyscraper construction in the earthquake-prone Japanese archipelago was "flexible structure."

Previously it was thought that a "rigid structure" embodied in sturdy, squat buildings was the safest way to combat the earthquake threat. But sweeping advances in seismological research clarified several vital points. For example, it was learned that earthquake undulations travel up and down buildings in wave-like patterns, and that because higher buildings require more time for this process to occur, the initial force of the shock waves gradually declines along with their destructive potential. Accordingly, if the quake waves could be entirely absorbed and cast off through a whip-like phenomenon — through a "flexible structure" — high-rise buildings could be erected in safety.

An old lesson was thus reconfirmed by the results of this research: the ancient craftsmen had already put the theory of "flexible construction" to practical use in building their pagodas. Professor Muto notes:

"They knew from experience that this would help absorb the energy of the quake to prevent a pagoda from collapsing."

Muto headed up the design team which built Japan's first high-rise building — the Kasumigaseki Building in downtown Tokyo, completed in 1968 and standing 147 meters with 36 stories. The skyscraper boom then accelerated rapidly, and as of December 1982 there were 50 buildings in Japan over 100 meters high, topped by the "Sunshine 60" building in the Ikebukuro district of Tokyo, 226 meters high with 60 stories above ground.

It took over a millenium, but now "pagodas" both of wood and steel tower together in the skies over Japanese soil.

Old wooden pagoda at Ueno in Tokyo.

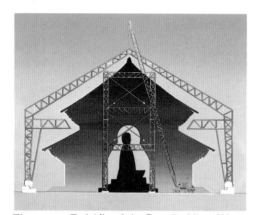

During repairs, Todai-ji was covered by the *suyane*.

The *suyane*, Todai-ji and the Great Buddha of Nara.

Modern Technology Revives the Ancient

Nara is home to the world's *oldest* wooden structure, Horyu-ji, and the world's *largest* wooden structure, Todai-ji, the temple housing the Great Buddha. The temple stands 57 meters wide, 50.5 meters deep and 47.34 meters high. Enshrined within this huge building is the 16-meter-high image of the Great Buddha Vairocana, the world's largest cast-metal figure.

Records reveal, however, that two years after this Buddha was consecrated in 752, a temple designed to surround the structure was built to a span almost 30 meters wider than the present one. The temple burned to the ground twice during civil wars, and today's Todai-ji dates from the early 18th century.

The most recent repair project on the temple was launched in the spring of 1973. Shimizu Construction Company, one of the nation's premier builders of high-rises, won the contract for this huge project, thus putting state-of-the-art construction technology to work in the repair of an ancient wooden structure.

The highlight of the project was the assembly of the *suyane*, a temporary steel roof erected to cover and protect the actual temple roof during the repair work. The decision to launch the repair effort in the first place was prompted by the severe leakage of the existing roof.

The construction of the *suyane* began with assembly of a steel scaffold frame at the right flank of the building. When this was completed, railroad tracks were laid at both the front and rear of the temple. Then steel rollers were placed on the tracks, and, enlisting the additional strength of a hydraulic jack at the base of the scaffold, the entire structure was slid atop the rollers horizontally until it literally covered the temple. Utilizing this frame, construction of the *suyane* was completed — the final version stood 55 meters high and weighed 2,300 tons. Inside the metal cover one construction elevator, two chain conveyors and five cranes were installed for the subsequent roof repair work.

The roof tiles received especially close attention, as the major cause of the rain leakage was the reduced number of tiles used in the last repair work, conducted in the Meiji era — the idea to reduce the weight burden on the roof had backfired. The Shimizu engineers racked their brains for a way to increase the number of

Ornamental tile atop Todai-ji — 3.4 meters high, copper covered with gold leaf.

tiles above that used back in Meiji while holding the aggregate weight to the existing tonnage.

While about 40 percent of the old tile was used in the revamped roof, new tile sections were hollowed out about one centimeter on their undersides, reducing their weight by 1.5 kilograms per section. Furthermore, the method of packing earth under concave roof tiles was updated by substituting two lengths of resin piping for half the earth. But there was still work ahead: to combat the danger of rainwater collecting at and then permeating tile joints, each tile was made six centimeters longer than before, while small drain grooves were opened near each joint. But it was still necessary to keep the water flowing along the tiles until it fell from the roof. To do this, an ingenious plan was adopted in which small upturned copper plates were placed beneath the overhang of each tile to collect the water, then allow it to flow over the surface of the next tile. This process was repeated at each tile section until the water was channeled into drain gutters at the edge of the roof, with about 110,000 roof tiles eventually set in this fashion.

This mammoth repair project enlisted the expertise of temple carpenters and a broad range of other craftsmen to carefully handle each phase of the work, whether major or minor. In all, over 100,000 persons were directly involved.

Yukuo Yagi (1942-), the Shimizu engineer and director of the Todai-ji project, reminisces about their role in the restoration:

"Construction work on ancient temples and shrines involves digging directly to the roots of Japanese culture, to restore and preserve them for the future. I want people a century from now to gaze upon our work, and say with conviction that the craftsmen of Showa (the current historical age dating from 1926) did a fine job."

The Todai-ji repair project was completed in the spring of 1980. Before their final departure, Yagi and his crew placed two apple crates in the attic cavity of the finished roof. These crates contain a scale model and documents describing the *suyane* roof "slide technique," tile design diagrams, assorted measuring devices such as rulers and leveling strings, and other items utilized in the construction — a small offering to future craftsmen, showing the pride which artisans of the 20th century took in their work.

After seven years of reconstruction, the Todai-ji is once again consecrated.

SCULPTURE

HORU
"To Carve"

Horin Matsuhisa, Japan's premiere Buddhist image maker.

Three Generations of Buddhist Image Makers

Enshrined within Nara's Todai-ji temple is a gilt bronze Buddha standing 16 meters high. This "Great Buddha" was reconstructed during the Edo period, but it is said that when originally consecrated in the eighth century, it was covered with gold leaf, and emitted a spectacular radiance when touched by the light of the sun.

In eighth-century Japan there were no craftsmen capable of sculpting such a gigantic image, and Chinese experts were asked to oversee the work. The Yamato Court strengthened its claims on national sovereignty using the doctrines of Buddhism imported from China via the Korean peninsula. One related result was rapid advances in Buddhist sculpture, using a wide range of materials including metal, stone and wood.

However, once this foreign cultural entity took root and the age of simple imitation passed, the Japanese taste swung overwhelmingly to favor wooden carvings. This trend has continued to this day, and now nine of ten Buddhist images produced are made of wood. Even today, about 100 craftsmen still dedicate their lives to the creation of fine wooden Buddhas.

Born in 1901, Horin Matsuhisa is Japan's oldest Buddhist image maker. In the 70 years since he received his first carving knife from his foster father, Horin has created over 4,000 images.

One of this master's favorite practice methods involves carving intricate geometric patterns into wood. Quadrangles, ovals and rhombuses are carved and combined into complex flower-shaped images, with more successful examples often used by Horin for the pedestals upon which his carved Buddhas sit. This is the very first carving technique that the young Horin learned from his foster father. He describes this particular phase of his craft:

"To create these patterns, straight, curved and slanted lines are intertwined. By doing this, it becomes easier to learn the basics of how to use carving tools properly. The skill of the carver can be clearly appraised by examining what the chisel edge leaves behind — wood tells no lies. The time and skill dedicated to a carving tell a true tale on the finished wood surface, meaning that the artist must at all times strive to be one with his work."

Inspired by this philosophy, Horin, although

well over 80, diligently carries on the skill-polishing technique learned early in childhood.

Horin's son Sorin (1926-) began to work under his father in his late teens and is now an excellent Buddhist image maker in his own right. Working out of a studio located in the suburbs of Kyoto, Sorin teaches his art to about a dozen apprentice carvers, and is now in the midst of a project which calls for building five Dharani, one major school of Buddhist images distinguished by their fearful countenances inspired by fifth-century sutras. To be six meters tall at completion, they will be the largest of their kind in Japan. Sorin's studio is outfitted with a ceiling-mounted crane to move images around, jacks and other modern tools reminding a visitor more of an ironworks than an artist's atelier.

The actual technology currently utilized for crafting Buddhist images, however, is a mosaic-type wood marquetry process introduced in the 14th century. The wood of many trees is used as the basic material. Sorin's current project utilizes about 20 six- to seven-meter lengths of 300-year-old *hinoki* root wood.

The creation process begins with the construction of a one-fifth scale prototype. A set number of *hinoki* blocks are covered on all sides with a highly systematic dotted grid pattern drawn in indelible India ink, then glued together to form a single larger wood block. The one-meter-high prototype image is sculpted from this block. After completion it is lowered into a tub of boiling water, allowing the glue to melt and the image to break apart into its composite blocks. Remaining, however, is the ink grid, which shows the lines and curves of the carving, and the distances between individual grid dots are used to compute the exact measurements of the larger image. This is an extremely logical method relying upon "three dimensional graph paper" which results when the prototype is separated into its original members.

Even after a full day at his studio spent guiding his apprentices, in the evenings Sorin carves diligently on a one-meter statue in the workshop of his own home.

"True wood carving begins when the wood, the artist and the tool become one. The artist adds his spirit, and the wood is transformed into a single image. This is the fascinating part. Some may believe that traditional craftsmanship seeks only to preserve ancient shapes and form.

A Buddhist image created by Horin, his son Sorin and his granddaughter Maya.

In his free time Sorin carves images at home.

Sorin carving one of five Dharani to be the largest of their kind in Japan.

Kirigane, a gluing art revived by Maya Matsuhisa.

The tools of *kirigane* (from the left): bamboo tube, bamboo tweezers, brushes and glue.

Maya's hands move with swift accuracy to lay gold leaf patterns.

However, I do not consider myself restricted by traditional Buddhism or any other frame of reference."

Slightly removed from the strict "professionalism" of his father, Sorin has discovered a new sense of purpose as a Buddhist image maker — drawn from the enjoyment, the stimulation of the carving process itself.

Sorin's daughter Maya (1954-) has carried this traditional art even closer to the modern. Her forte is *kirigane* — the fine art of cutting and placing gold leaf — an intricate skill which only five living Japanese have developed to the artisan level. Thin gold leaf is cut into string-like lengths, then attached to a Buddhist image with special glue to form the garb of the Buddha.

Maya kneels in traditional Japanese style before an unpainted Buddhist image, clothed in a white organdy blouse and a tight-fitting skirt. She grips a brush in each hand, the left-hand brush lifting a length of gold leaf and the right-hand brush dipped in the glue. After holding them both motionless in the air for several breathless moments, she lays the golden leaf upon the statue, applying the glue immediately to hold it in place. The right-hand brush is then removed to sever the string at the desired point. After countless repetitions magnificent gold-leaf patterns arise on the surface of the *hinoki* Buddha. The sleeves of Maya's blouse swell out as she works. Soon they dance with sparkling bits of gold leaf that have escaped from her brush.

"The qualities of gold are not well represented by either India ink or pencil, and as a result, I never preface my work with any sort of rough sketch. *Kirigane* is an instant, extemporaneous art form — a design approach whose success or failure is determined by the sharpness of the lines as they are laid."

Maya is responsible for introducing circular lines into the *kirigane* process — a practice once considered a taboo in this highly traditional art. She has also forsaken charcoal as the chief means of applying the gold leaf, in favor of "a more common tool which anyone can get their hands on" — the iron.

Artists spanning three generations — Horin, Sorin and Maya. Traditions passed on, renewed and enhanced, until a new tradition is given life.

Young Restorers of Culture

Utilizing their backgrounds in the modern tradition of fine arts, there are young artists who strive to breathe new life into proven classical techniques. Some like Maya Matsuhisa, above, move from traditional indoctrinations into new, experimental art forms. Others, educated with totally modern backgrounds, use their education as a springboard to return to the traditional.

One of the latter is Fumiya Odaya (1941-) who together with interested artists established the "Tokyo Cultural Treasure Restoration Center." Through this Center, Odaya has organized the restoration of over 70 Buddhist images, and is now engaged in the dismantling and repair of three images (one Buddha and two guardian Deva kings) at Shuzen-ji, a well-known temple in the Izu Peninsula about three hours' drive from Tokyo.

These images are believed to date from the 14th to 15th centuries, and were consecrated as offerings for the happiness of the second Kamakura *shogun*. They were crafted through intricate marquetry craftsmanship, with an astounding 2,000 components used to build each small, 203-centimeter-tall image.

The restoration project began with the dismantling of all wooden components. They were laid out side by side, and holes left by insects were impregnated with a special resin filler. The lacquer and glue used for bonding were dried and eventually fell off as a powder.

From time to time faults develop in an image. In the Shuzen-ji repairs, for example, Odaya found it necessary to replace the right leg of one of the Deva guardians. While antique colors were added to avoid an unnatural finish, future researchers will be able to tell at a glance that repairs were once made. Odaya comments on the process:

"Our restoration is concerned primarily with strengthening the statues to help preserve them for future generations."

However, after removal of all dirt and stains and completion of repairs, the images were completely restored to their original appearance. It is believed that ancient Buddhist images were constructed on the premise that they would be so dismantled and restored at least once every century. The completion of the image is considered a beginning, not a conclusion.

Fumiya Odaya, a man dedicated to restoring ancient images.

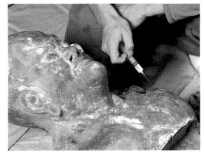

A guardian Deva king from the 14th or 15th century. Its age may be ascertained by external appearance.

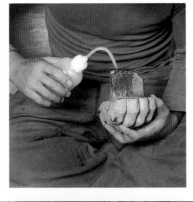

The statue's foot is reinforced by impregnating it with a resin filler.

Dismantling alone often requires six months.

SWORDS

KITAERU
"To Forge"

The Dream of a Living National Treasure

Freezing winds from Siberia blowing across the Japan Sea to Japan's Hokuriku district announce the arrival of winter.

At least one person welcomes this cold weather, because it heralds the season during which he can most easily immerse himself in his craft. He is Seiho Sumitani (1921-), a "living national treasure" in the art of forging traditional Japanese swords. His workshop is located in Matsuto, a small city slightly inland from the Japan Sea.

Japanese swords are distinguished by the curvature of their blades, as well as the beautiful texture of their steel and the intricate engraved designs. The intrinsic value of these swords comes from these three qualities, the degree of which is determined almost solely by the forging skills of the swordsmith.

While the standard Western sword is formed from a single steel, Japanese swords are forged from a combination of sheet steel, soft steel and pig iron or cast steel, distinguished by their different carbon contents.

Sumitani's workshop is dimly lit, with a high ceiling and a single tiny window. Dark purple smoke from Japanese red pine charcoal rises murkily into the air, and as a bone-chilling wind

Master swordsmith Seiho Sumitani.

Sword-honing master Kokei Ono.

Scabbard-making expert Kazuyuki Takayama.

A sword and its Itomaki furniture of Fukuoka Ichimon-ji.

rages against the outside walls, Sumitani braces his sinewy body as he turns to the charcoal fire. He lifts out a hunk of red-hot steel, wraps it in Japanese rice paper, and douses it with muddy water mixed with clay. The next step calls for application of straw ash over the entire length, which is then cast back into the coals. The water and ash prevent the steel surface from over-heating, thereby keeping the entire fragment from growing too hot and oxidizing — which would greatly weaken the strength of the blade to be formed.

After 30 minutes the metal is retrieved from the fire. Sumitani pounds it first with a small hammer, then with a larger one rigged to run mechanically. This pounding extends the length of the steel, and after a special chisel is used to make a cut in the middle the hot metal is folded in half and stuck back together to restore the substance to its original length. This process is repeated again and again, and the weight of the steel is gradually reduced from its original weight of over nine kilograms to just under one kilogram. The weight loss is accounted for by the impurities and carbon extracted in the process.

This particular forging technique is the secret of Japan's superbly tempered swords. Sumitani stares intently at the color of both the hot steel and the fire, and adjusts the coals as he sees fit. To enhance visibility at this vital phase of the work he allows no superfluous lighting in his workshop, and has removed all flourescent bulbs. It is important that even the smallest hair-like flaw in the steel not escape his eye, and as Sumitani jumps nimbly around the fire he peers penetratingly into the soul of his "living steel."

"Good eyes and stamina are the key to this technology. Once they are gone so is the art, and the challenge is to create the sword desired while I am still in top health."

The core of the blade is forged in the above fashion, blending pig iron and sheet steel. Then comes the creation of the blade coating, which is forged in much the same way, but using soft iron and sheet steel. The finished blade is eventually sandwiched firmly into the heated coating, which is then hammered into a perfect fit. This softer coating greatly enhances the rigidity of the blade inside, creating a sword which is able to withstand stronger impact and is less likely to break than swords built through western forging processes.

Japan's traditional swordsmiths have used the softer outside coating of their swords to perfect

The swordsmith heats the steel for hours to strengthen its mettle.

The honing master carefully chooses the exact type of whetstone needed.

the wavy decorative patterns that appear on the blades. Once the insertion of the blade in its sleeve and subsequent shaping have been completed, a special blend of straw ash and red mud is applied to the blade's surface, and allowed to dry. A bamboo spatula is then used to etch designs through the dried mud substance and into the blade, which is then returned to the fire. Patterns conceived by the swordsmith are thus carved and baked into the steel finish, and appear in their full splendor when the blade is first polished. The ultimate aim of the master swordsmith is not only to forge strong, useful swords, but also to make them pleasing to the eye.

This special tempering process to the blade itself creates the distinctive "warp" of Japanese swords. This particular shape is reminiscent of similarly curved bits of Japanese culture – the eaves of traditional houses, stone walls, the Japanese *kana* script and so forth. The classical Japanese sense saw vulgarity in creating a strong, keen-edged sword designed only with practical use in mind. Delicate curves were thus added to formerly straight blades in careful attempts to refine the sheer strength of a sword with aesthetic elegance.

While Sumitani has already been designated a living national treasure in his field, there is still one personal dream he says he has yet to attain – to bring back to life the ancient brand of Japanese sword-making which reached its zenith in the mid-12th century. Although he feels he has moved within "one step" of achieving this goal, he claims there is still a certain small area where his understanding is not yet complete. Without this final missing link, he says it will be impossible to pass on this unsurpassed 12th century forging process to the present and future generations.

With this one thought in mind, Seiho Sumitani races against time. Will the years remaining to him be sufficient to fill the gaps in technology and time?

The Master Honer and Scabbard Maker

The blades that leave Seiho Sumitani's workshop are far from being finished Japanese swords. There is a saying that "a sword's value is determined in equal degrees by both its quality and the honing of the blade." In other words, a good blade is only as good as its sharpener.

Kokei Ono (1912-) is also a "living national treasure" in the field of sword honing. He resides in a quiet seaside town outside of Tokyo.

Six types of whetstones are used in the honing of Japanese swords, in a process of moving to progressively finer degrees of sharpness and polish. Ono examines the texture and pattern of a blade, working on three-centimeter sections at a time. It is vital, he says, to maintain a near-perfect balance between the right and left hand; if this balance is interrupted, for even an instant, the blade may be permanently scarred. Ono claims he can spot the competence of a sword honer simply by how he holds himself, seated before a blade to apply the intricate tools of his trade.

Ono reaches the final honing stage, sliding thinly cut whetstones mounted on his fingertips along the shining blade skin. When this fine polishing work is done, he holds the blade at a horizontal angle, to let the sunlight fall softly upon each and every millimeter of his effort.

"No two swords are alike. Each possesses its own face, its own personality. The true goal of sword honing is to draw forth the highest essence of each blade, and to exhibit to the naked eye the ultimate beauty, the ultimate luster inherent in the steel finish."

The final stage of its evolution demands a craftsman who will enhance the beauty of the polished blade with an exquisite casing.

Kazuyuki Takayama (1940-) is the latest in a long line of scabbard artisans. In his backyard he maintains a regular stock of magnolia logs. In order to form a scabbard he sculpts two magnolia lengths to fit the curve of the blade, then glues them together. The adhesive used is a light-strength paste created by mashing cooked rice with a bamboo spatula into a smooth, consistent blend. Heavy-strength gluing agents are rejected in consideration of future rust-related repairs: While effectively cementing the two halves together, the rice paste adhesive also makes it possible to pull them apart without damaging the wood surface.

The ultimate secret in this craft is to create the sensation that the sword is touching evenly all along the inside of the scabbard, when in fact it is only in stronger contact at the hilt. If any part of the blade itself is allowed to come into more firm contact, the moisture from the wood will cause rust. Since experts like Takayama have mastered this technique, however, in a sense the use of the rice paste is unnecessary as subsequent repairs to prevent rust will probably never be necessary. But tradition is tradition, and the use of this paste is an institution which continues to be emphasized as a key element in scabbard making.

Takayama appears to perform his craft with exaggerated ease. He commented on this point:

The scabbard maker uses 15 different planes to create a perfect fit.

"With a truly excellent sword, I hold scabbard crafting to a minimum. The key is to create a natural shape which will enhance the beauty and warp of the blade itself. I often examine scabbards I have made in the past, and at times find them unnatural. At those times I feel that, perhaps, I have been making progress in my art."

Sword-making is truly a team effort, involving swordsmith, blade honer and scabbard craftsman. When these three artists successfully blend their talents in a spirit of mutual harmony and understanding, the result is a sublime beauty.

POTTERY

YAKU
"To Fire"

Kakiemon Sakaida, 14th generation master, sketches a flower.

Handing Down Secrets

Arita, a small town in Saga Prefecture in Kyushu, Japan's major southern isle, is the nation's ceramics capital. Arita is home to over 150 workshops, and the town is particularly distinguished by its time-honored custom of passing skills from father to son. Whether it be the potter's wheel or the painter's brush, an Arita family engaged in one of the traditional arts can generally trace its history back several generations.

Japan was the last part of Asia to develop its own pottery tradition, and the first distinctively Japanese porcelain can be traced to the kilns of Arita. The greater Saga area was known as Hizen during Japan's feudal age, and as the region was the closest geographically to the Asian mainland, there was a constant inflow of cultural objects, including beautiful porcelain pieces from China and Korea, entering through the port of Hirado. While these specimens tantalized the artistic imaginations of Japan's would-be potters, they had little clue of the processes which led to their creation.

The mainstream of Japanese pottery had been ceramics. In simple terms, the major difference between ceramics and porcelain is the materials used and firing temperatures. While ceramics consist principally of clay and are fired at about 1,000 degrees centigrade, porcelain is made essentially from finely crushed kaolin, quartz and feldspar stone and is fired at temperatures above 1,300 degrees.

Conflicts between different peoples and nations often open the door to technological exchange. Porcelain was one such example for Japan. Hideyoshi Toyotomi (1536-1598), the powerful generalissimo who largely unified Japan during the latter half of the 16th century, led a futile military expedition to Korea during his reign, and many Korean artisans were taken to Japan with him. Among these craftsmen was a ceramist named Lee Sanpei.

Lee decided to stay in Japan, and in the early 17th century discovered porcelain stone deposits on Izumiyama, a mountain in the Arita district, suited for the pure white chinaware that was his specialty back in Korea. He proceeded to successfully develop a ceramic technology using this stone.

Once the potters of Arita had mastered the

Kaki (Japanese persimmon) tree in Kakiemon's garden.

white porcelain technique, they turned to imitating and then surpassing the colored enamelling that had reached its zenith in mid-16th century China. This cherished dream was soon achieved by a master named Kakiemon Sakaida in about 1642, striking the keynote for future generations of Arita artisans.

Nearly three and a half centuries later, Tadashi Sakaida (1934-) appeared at the Arita City Hall to notify the authorities of his intention to change his name to Kakiemon Sakaida. His father Kakiemon, the 13th generation in a continuing line of ceramists, had passed away, transferring the custody of the family tradition to his son.

From its very first generation, the Sakaida family feared that the secret of its floral enamelling technology, developed by the first Kakiemon, would escape from the family's realm, and a strict custom of passing on the methods solely to the eldest son was started. All other sons were adopted into other families — an example of the uncompromising inheritance system which characterizes the artisan society of Arita.

Still active porcelain stone deposits discovered on Izumiyama by Lee Sanpei.

The current Kakiemon comments: "It might seem ridiculous to guard these secrets for 14 generations. But we view this as the only truly reliable method of a cultural transmission." He explains that while certainly not every generation produces outstanding advances in the ceramic art, the practice of giving gifted children special training dramatically increases the odds that a true master will emerge — one of the main reasons for the consistently superior level of Arita porcelain. Kakiemon points to "Kakiemon copies" in German Meissenware and Dutch Delftware as evidence of the excellent reputation of his family's tradition and the influence it has had globally.

Pottery apprentices work hard to become masters as the Arita legacy is passed on.

One of the true masters was the current Kakiemon's father — the 13th generation Kakiemon (1906 - 1982). Working with his own father (the 12th generation master), this Kakiemon succeeded in reviving a "cream glaze" ceramic method which had lain dormant for over two centuries. Porcelain created in this style greatly enhanced the fine lines of Kakiemon's colorful enamels, and made optimum use of the remaining whitish space. Resembling the milky white color of water used to wash rice, the hue and texture of porcelain created through

In the pursuit of excellence over half of all work is discarded.

this method lifted the color contrasts of the world of pottery to a new high.

The resurrection of this ancient cream glaze technique gained the 13th generation Kakiemon designation as a living national treasure. His son, however, spoke of his serious concern about the future of his art.

"This technique cannot be carried on by our family alone. The roots are far-reaching, and stretch to the clay makers, brush makers, enamel blenders and other craftsmen. Without expertise at each of these levels the porcelain cannot be finished, and I am worried about our ability to maintain the intricate ties that are the key to sustained success."

In a word, the cream glaze porcelain process must be expertly orchestrated by Kakiemon, with guidance given to all who must participate in the process. Let's take a brief look at how the work is organized. It begins with making the clay itself.

First, an expert capable of removing impurities from the porcelain stone must be found. Three special types of stone found in the Arita area are crushed separately into powders. Water is then added and the fine particles which rise to the top of the liquid go into separate vats.

The next stage involves an artisan skilled in bringing the three solutions to optimum consistency. Working directly under Kakiemon, he dips broken porcelain chips of the desired thickness into each vat, and examines the mud-like liquid sticking to the chip to see if it dries to the correct thickness. Kakiemon keeps a close watch, and orders the addition of water to the blend at times when he feels the solution is too thick.

When the three solutions reach the same consistency they are combined. Then the thick liquid is poured into a stone tub with sand and straw matting in the bottom to remove the water. A thick white sediment remains on the top of the matting — the clay used in the cream glaze technique. The workmen continue to knead and stir until the clay becomes sticky and viscous, and then transfer the material to the potter's wheel.

The next important step in the process is the application of a white glaze to the fired pottery. Bark and leaf ash from the *yusu,* a tree indigenous to Japan, is used to make this glaze, because of its high lime content. This ash is

Reds are the hallmark of Kakiemon's work.

purchased by apple-crate lot through a special supplier, although after testing usually only about three or four handfuls from each load can actually be used for the glaze. When the glaze has been applied and the pieces fired again, the distinctive creamy color after which the process is named appears on the porcelain.

Kakiemon then turns to the delicate painting process which, more than anything else, distinguishes his family's pottery. The paint used to produce his reds receives particular care. Red oxide of iron is burned to a powder and then left in hot water for over a year to remove all ash and impurities. After this period, the solution is carefully agitated until it separates into three levels: the finer particles at the top known as "flower red" are used to paint the most delicate parts of the flower; the medium-level particles known as "deep red" are used to depict the fuller areas of petals and stems; and the coarser particles at the bottom known as "line drawing red" are used for the least delicate contours of the flower.

A major challenge that the 14th generation Kakiemon will face is the transmission of the cream glaze porcelain technique to a successor, a task which will require major expenditures of time and the organization of expert assistance at every phase of the process. The Kakiemon pottery tradition is not one of gaudy, ornamental porcelain. Rather, the aim is for common, practical ware which can be used in everyday life. This has led to a persistent dedication to simple, clear technique, featuring ample white spaces, and accented by equally simple floral patterns. This ware lends itself to almost any situation, and his dream is to put new thought and spirit into his family's tradition of common, yet exquisite porcelain.

He has always loved to roam through fields, sketching the strong, powerful lines of the flowers blooming there. He was particularly drawn to chrysanthemums, peonies and plums, and these are the blossoms that now adorn the graceful simplicity of his work.

Cream glaze porcelain is a technique now practiced exclusively by Kakiemon. As he drew closer to succession to his professional name, this 14th generation artisan peered intently into the faces of flowers, pondering how his own art would enhance the creamy rice-water-like hue resurrected by his father after so many decades.

A Kakiemon masterpiece
– "Strawberry Flowers" –
45 centimeters in diameter.

"Noriutsugi" vase, with a diameter of 25 centimeters.

Thirteenth generation master Imaemon Imaizumi mixes colors in the classic method.

A Division of Labor

The fame of Arita porcelain spread quickly. The Dutch East India Company exported various pieces to Europe beginning in the mid-17th century, gaining a great following. These importers dubbed it "Old Imari," which it is still called today because the shipments were loaded at Imari, the port city closest to Arita. In contrast to the landlocked "Silk Road," Arita ware compiled an illustrious history by moving along a "Ceramic Road" sea route from Japan, to China, around India and finally to Europe.

The Nabeshima clan, which dominated the greater Arita district, worked hard to maintain good kilns to turn out top-quality porcelain. In the kilns operated directly by clan authorities a special brand of porcelain originated, initially developed as offerings and gifts for the Imperial Family and the *daimyo* (feudal lords). Now known as Nabeshima ware, pieces with the designs and colors distinguishing this ceramic technique are recognized as one of the true peaks of Japanese porcelain.

Dwelling in a sturdy wooden house built in the declining years of the Edo period, Imaemon Imaizumi (1926-), a 13th generation master, is the only living person capable of creating colored-picture-designed Nabeshima ware. His ancestors served successively as the official ceramics painters of the Nabeshima clan, and the secrets of concocting the special paints used in the process have been carefully protected, passing them on to only one child in each generation. To this day, Imaemon keeps the vital details of the process locked in a cabinet in his home. Ranking alongside Kakiemon as one of Arita's representative artisans, Imaemon also owes his success to this time-honored guarding of artistic secrets.

Nevertheless, the styles of Kakiemon and Imaemon represent opposite poles of the art form. While the former's worship of natural beauty is reflected in articulately simple enameled floral designs, the painting of Imaemon seeks to push art to a further potential, pursuing pure, absolute beauty in a world of immaculate refinement.

Imaemon's workshop is a living relic of the Nabeshima clan. Male workers sit by the east window, using the sunlight that flows through the clear glass to illuminate their desks. Across

Male-female division of labor — with different color slippers.

the room, with their backs to the men, are female workers painting pieces with thicker brushes. The Arita tradition favors teamwork, with men painting the line designs and women in charge of the dye application. The difficulty of the work is comparable, and there is no difference in male and female wage scales.

The system is a highly efficient division of labor, but not a rationalization program aimed at any modernizing method; each step of the process is a time-demanding tradition in itself, making it next to impossible to trade off jobs. Each craftsman is equal to others in his or her relationship with Imaemon, and the master functions much like a movie director as he orchestrates the work, drawing a wide group of artists together. And like a skillfully directed film, the final results reflect Imaemon's particular standards of excellence.

In a sense, this excellence depends heavily on the skilled craftsmen who work with him. This means that top-flight artisans are indispensable to the next generation.

"The skills which are hammered into the mind, into the hands of the craftsman since childhood are not something which fail with age. The key is desire. A child who has attained journeyman skills may see his own grandmother doing the same work and tell her to quit, because it is 'unsightly' for an old lady to be working. I tell the child to let her work as long as she wants if he is really interested in filial piety. Wanting to work is a vital element."

In accordance with this ethic, even though Imaemon pays his workers a lump retirement sum at the age of 65, those who want to continue may do so, with no reduction in pay.

While it might appear that Imaemon is comfortably supported by this system, which offers generous benefits to skilled craftspersons, in fact he stands quite alone.

"Simply bringing to life the old designs is not enough. We will only be upstaged in the end by the older pieces themselves. We must forever push ahead, working in the cradle of tradition as we pioneer new methods, new designs."

Imaemon struggles daily to balance his love of both old and new, entranced by the mystical art of faraway Egypt and the Middle East, surrounded by the relics of 13 generations of Nabeshima excellence.

A 13th generation Imaemon masterpiece: "Iro-Nabeshima Light Lapis Pampas Grass" (bowl, diameter 42 centimeters).

"Light India Ink Grass with Dew" (large bowl, diameter at mouth 37 centimeters).

"Iro-Nabeshima Lotus on Green" (vase, diameter 19 centimeters).

Chuemon Okugawa, second generation master at work on porcelain.

A delicate porcelain pattern — the sole decoration on an otherwise plain surface.

Creating the exact lines desired while the clay still lives.

The Master of "Old Imari"

Growing around the old wooden home of Kakiemon are *kaki* (Japanese persimmon) trees dating back to the Edo period; if one stands on the dirt floor of Imaemon's house and gazes straight up, a thick, darkly gleaming beam is seen stretching overhead, a strong, silent statement of a sturdy, time-honored tradition.

Yet another Arita master, second generation Chuemon Okugawa (1930-), can be found in an entirely different environment. He lives a solitary existence, alone with his pottery tools in a modest hut facing a rice paddy.

Chuemon is not part of a long, continuing line of artisans like the masters we have discussed so far. His tradition originates with the greatness of his father, who, dedicating himself to the "Old Imari" school, created exceptional techniques in this forgotten and highly specialized type of porcelain. His pieces are large dishes and bowls about 60 centimeters in diameter, as well as tall jars as high as 150 centimeters. The approach itself is in contrast to the mainstream Arita tradition of colorful painting, accenting instead elegant forms using a clear white finish on the oversized pieces.

The current Chuemon reminisces about his father:

"In the old days we had only pedal-operated potter's wheels, and my father often made me crawl under the contraption and turn it by hand. He would get very wound up in his work, and at times yelled at me that I wasn't turning hard enough. Sometimes I'd even get a kick in the pants. The wheels to sculpt big pieces really do require two people to operate, and I thought many times that it just wasn't worth the sweat and strain needed to succeed."

The sweat and strain of a potter tackling such large pieces are indeed impressive. Even with the most carefully selected materials, clay can be expected to yield overly flat or swollen lines. But Chuemon strictly observes the teaching of his father that "the life of a piece of pottery is in the base and the mouth," and works diligently to eliminate any trace of warp. The wheel is used to form mouths which open with the elegance and grace of a flower in bloom, petal-like edges which curve back elegantly toward the body of the piece, and other demanding touches. The fine lines that stretch harmoniously from the base to the mouth are testimony to Chuemon's dedicated refusal to stray from the original form or compromise to any degree whatsoever his pursuit of perfection.

The big 150 centimeter jars are finished in three separate sections. Chuemon creates each part with equal care, bringing to life the wheel techniques passed down by his father. As if a living organism, the clay rapidly changes in consistency. Moisture rises from its depths and the resulting natural change in weight causes distortion. Chuemon turns his wheel repeatedly, reshaping the hardening substance constantly.

The master casts his eyes around his workshop hut, keeping a close watch on all three sections and waiting for the single best moment to join them together. If this step is carried out too early, the clay will warp and distort. Waiting too long will allow hardening which renders final adjustments impossible. But the years have taught Chuemon well. The magic moment arrives, and like a painter whose only tool of measurement is his keen eye, Chuemon interlocks all three pieces so expertly they blend without a trace of distortion or jointing.

The design blueprints are locked somewhere deep in his mind, and like a well-programmed computer with systems functioning perfectly, Chuemon creates a study in symmetrical perfection: the right- and left-side curves and arcs of the jar stand together in a breathless balance of superb harmony.

Chuemon's fingertips are as soft as a baby's, and he uses their sensitive touch to test the moisture in his clay, keeping the dryness and thickness to just the right degree, pushing and reforming the substance just before distortion sets in. Step by step, the jar assumes its large, yet finely detailed form. Chuemon's computer "eye" uses the tender flesh in his fingers as a sensor to gather the data necessary for greatness.

The technical expertise of Arita runs deep. Chuemon is yet another artisan who has dedicated his life to artistic tradition, to restoring fine crafts and techniques which have begun to fade from the workshops of modern-day Japan.

Second generation Chuemon porcelain masterpiece (vase, diameter 29 centimeters).

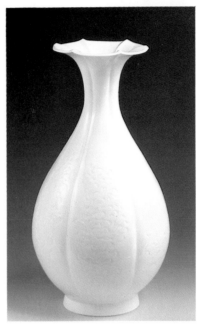

White porcelain with peonies and lilies (vase, diameter 29 centimeters).

White porcelain (vase, diameter 41 centimeters).

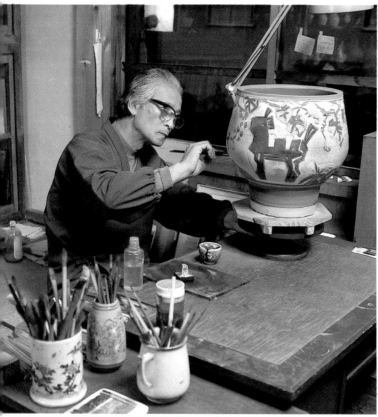
Fujio Kitade, absorbed in his painting late at night.

Closeup of the master's finely detailed work.

Techniques Nurtured by the Cold

Kutani, a small town in Ishikawa Prefecture, lies approximately 750 kilometers northeast of Arita. This is the Hokuriku region of Japan, which in direct contrast to the warm, comfortable environs of Kyushu suffers from heavy snowfalls, as it borders the Japan Sea. In the not-so-distant past the people of this region would spend most of their time from December through March, and sometimes even April, cloistered inside their homes, peering through window panes onto endless white landscapes, awaiting the first traces of spring.

It is said that a certain samurai carried the knowledge of Arita ceramics to faraway Kutani in the latter part of the 17th century. Once implanted, the focus of the porcelain art form moved slightly seaward from Kutani proper, while the particular natural features of this region stimulated development of a distinctive pottery style. In due time, Kutani ware eventually came to be ranked with Arita porcelain for its artistic excellence. In contrast to the refined elegance of Arita pieces, however, the Kutani school is identified by strong, relaxed lines, in which can be read the rugged heartiness of the people of Kutani and of the Hokuriku region in general, who traditionally braved the cold, snowy winter months to welcome with wholehearted joy the arrival of spring.

The work of one of Japan's leading modern ceramists, Fujio Kitade (1919-), is an excellent example of the Kutani tradition of strength and purpose. Kitade's pieces are distinguished by his engraving and painting techniques, which eventually cover all traces of the original natural clay surface. Known as the "paint overlay" style, this method contrasts sharply with the Kakiemon school, which emphasizes ample use of whitish space to offset the design.

Kitade's Seisen (Blue Spring Kiln) faces out across a road to an expanse of rice paddies. In the rear, a dense forest reaches right up to the side of the building, concealing a number of natural woodburning kilns, which, although once the birthplace of many famous ceramic pieces, have now fallen into disuse and decay.

Even on Sunday, when his assistants do not come to the kiln, Kitade works on alone, diligently engraving and painting his work. When the sun goes down there are no street lamps to light the surrounding area, and a naked light bulb illuminating Kitade's workshop creates a floating silhouette of the master's form viewed from the outside darkness. Surrounded by the vast silence of the Hokuriku night, Kitade spoke of the essence of the Kutani painting tradition.

"Above all other things, the human eye is attracted to the world of *ao*. This is the mystical blue which weaves images of ocean depths, the dreamy green hue of new spring foliage. Delving even deeper, in my mind's eye, green is the key component of any color scheme."

The Japanese word *ao* describes a color which is interpreted sometimes as blue, and sometimes as green. For example, a Japanese will refer to both the color of the ocean and of foliage as *ao*. This linguistic interpretation may very well be yet another manifestation of the respect that the Japanese have toward nature, which is after all, the real source of all color. In any case, the works of Fujio Kitade are distinguished by the use of carefully mixed shades of blue and green to accent the engraved designs.

The Kitade tradition of painting over the clay surface with natural, living colors has been carried on for four generations, since the early Meiji period. The first two generations worked on a plain, natural finish, and then Fujio Kitade's father moved into carving and painting. As a result, the current master learned both schools, and is considered a rare talent in the natural finish approach as well.

The majority of pottery is formed on a wheel, sculpted upward to leave a hollow interior. The Kitade approach, however, involves engraving designs into the surface of a solid clay mass, using no pottery wheel. This is because applying carving tools to a piece which has already been hollowed could easily pierce through the sides and destroy the shape. Once the engraving is completed, inner clay is carefully removed to form the interior of the piece. Fujio Kitade was trained in this "sculpting out" process from boyhood, and has developed his own unique style of shaping.

The Kitade school breaks all pottery convention with its bold exterior engraving, and attractive *ao*-hued designs. A dimension much removed from the rigid tradition of Arita ware, this bold, freewheeling approach is yet another flower of Japanese ceramics, blooming in rugged snow-covered terrain.

Fujio Kitade masterpiece "Clear Day" (rounded jar, diameter 32 centimeters).

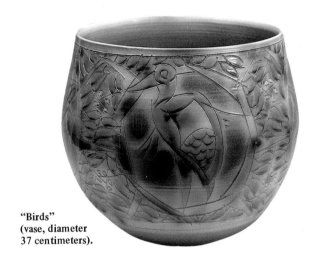

"Birds" (vase, diameter 37 centimeters).

"Repose" (diameter 32 centimeters).

The Ceramics Revolution

Earthenware, china, ceramics — the history of pottery reaches back more than 10,000 years. While the various types are classified by firing temperature, materials and other factors, all pottery consists of dirt, rock and similar materials, which are molded and fired to form finished pieces. Dishes, bowls, jars and many other items created in this fashion have been used as implements of everyday life for many centuries.

However, there is a more recent development in pottery which has created an entirely new and different category. This is the field of fine ceramics — an art which uses no clay, no stone. Highly purified nonferrous metals and other inorganic materials are carefully alloyed or refined, then fired at temperatures ranging from 1,500 to 2,000 degrees centigrade. The temperatures used with normal ceramics rarely rise above 1,400 degrees, so fine ceramics involves a totally new technology which exceeds the capabilities of manual processes — a new form of "pottery" made possible by scientific and technological advances.

Items produced in this fashion have excellent strength and durability, superb electric insulation and chemical-resistant properties, and lend themselves to finely detailed processing. As a result, they have become an indispensable part of integrated circuit packages and other sophisticated electronic components. New uses are being found daily. For example, fine ceramics are used in artificial tooth roots and bones, automotive parts and golf clubs.

Japan's foremost maker of fine ceramics is the Kyocera Corporation, headed by President Kazuo Inamori (1932-), a man with an engineering background. He started his own business, forming a small company with a total of 28 employees in 1959. Kyocera has now grown into a company with 8,000 employees.

Formerly it was known as Kyoto Ceramic Company, Ltd., and armed with business cards bearing this name, Inamori made the rounds of Japanese electronics makers. The first question was inevitably, "What is ceramics?" and when Inamori responded, "A type of porcelain," the reaction was usually a curt, "Sorry, we don't need any cups or bowls today."

But Inamori persevered. He announced that

President Kazuo Inamori of Kyocera Corporation in the company uniform.

he would attempt to make anything that other companies were unable to produce in-house. His confidence was based on the conviction that believing that something can be accomplished is vital, even if the actual possibility appears to be nil. He strives to instill the same belief in his employees, organizing them into small working groups known as "Amoebas," with one person taking full responsibility for the activities of each group. Furthermore, every worker has the opportunity for direct contact and communication with top management.

Inamori offered this summary of his management philosophy.

"Modern management technique tends to thrust aside all bothersome mental concerns, and concentrate instead on clear-cut, rational solutions for all situations. But a product created from sheer rationality will create little if any impression on the person who eventually uses it. In order to do work above and beyond the simple call of duty, one must participate wholeheartedly, both in heart and mind. The best means to discuss this and other important concerns with employees is certainly not through a confusing, bureaucratic organization. It is vital to take the time to talk in a one-on-one situation, with great candor and in great detail."

He used to both pay for and attend his company's annual "end-of-the-year party" in December — a gathering for workers to relax and enjoy themselves and a way of saying thanks for a year of hard work. While most Japanese company presidents refrain from appearing at these occasions, Inamori regarded it as an excellent opportunity for a friendly get-together and chat with his people.

The Kyocera practice favoring close ties between individual workers and the company president brings to mind the Nabeshima kiln of Imaemon Imaizumi. Imaemon does not run his organization with departments or sections. He treats all his craftsmen equally, and offers them advice not only about their work, but with regard to their private lives as well.

Fine ceramics, like any other form of pottery, involves hardening a substance and then firing it at high temperatures. This in turn causes the individual piece or component to contract by as much as 20 percent in length and 50 percent in cubic volume, a phenomenon which demands great attention to precision and detail.

Fiber-optic telecommunication connectors are a good example. These are minutely engineered components with an inner diameter of 126 microns, allowing a margin of error of only a single micron. In order to keep within such a tolerance, mind-boggling energy and concentration must be harnessed to develop tools which will hold deformation to an absolute minimum during the firing process. This is a form of "sculpting" which would present not a few problems even to the ceramics masters we have met earlier.

In such fashion, then, traditions move toward the future.

Fine ceramics are created at super-high temperatures.

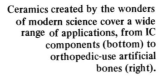

Ceramics created by the wonders of modern science cover a wide range of applications, from IC components (bottom) to orthopedic-use artificial bones (right).

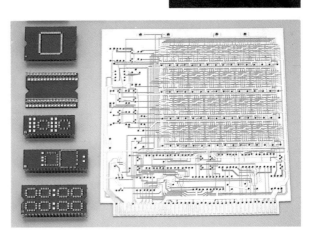

LACQUER

NURU
"To Lacquer, or Paint"

Hearts and Hands

Porcelain is "china" in English. And although not nearly as well-known, "japan" is a type of lacquer-coated ware. China was the cradle of porcelain-making and Japan is where the art of lacquering truly bloomed. Raw materials for lacquering come from the sap of the Japanese *urushi* (lacquer) tree, a deciduous variety found from northern Africa all the way to Japan. The highest quality *urushi,* however, comes from typhoon areas, which in this case means Korea, China and Japan. And among these three countries Japan is the prime target for these fierce tropical storms — so perhaps the top-quality *urushi* found there is a small gesture by nature to make amends.

Lacquer is a natural coating with a beautiful yet durable surface. It is also endowed with excellent adhesive properties. When these qualities are skillfully combined the result is fine lacquerware. Probably the best way to grasp the depths and possibilities inherent in this ancient art is to trace the footsteps of Japan's foremost living master in the field — Gonroku Matsuda (1896-).

Matsuda was born in Kanazawa, a city in the Hokuriku region of Japan where lacquerware has traditionally enjoyed great popularity. He first tried his hand at lacquering at the age of seven, working alongside a maker of Buddhist altars. By the time he graduated from a local technical high school, his skills were already well above average. Searching for a more academic approach to the magic of his art, Matsuda qualified for entrance to Tokyo National University of Fine Arts and Music, which was, and remains, the premier training ground for Japanese artists and musicians.

This was his springboard to greatness. After graduation, he was commissioned by a major Japanese fountain pen maker to create a pen with a gilded lacquer finish. This fountain pen became popular in Europe, where its rare esoteric lines made it an impressive instrument for signing important documents. Special sales contracts were closed with leading pen makers such as Dunhill and Maple. And orders for items with similar designs soon went beyond pens, expanding first to pipes and then to household decorations and tools.

Two of Matsuda's masterpieces are housed in

Gonroku Matsuda at work in his two-mat studio.

the National Diet Building — the artwork in a lounge and in the Imperial Family Room. Although completed in 1931, these pieces of lacquerware have the same strength and splendor as they did a half century ago, proving that the natural beauty of *urushi* lends itself to fine architecture as well. The walls of both the Upper and Lower Houses of the Diet are also finished with fine lacquer coatings applied by Matsuda's brushes.

Around the same time, the master also took on the challenge of decorating the doors of the first-class lounge of an ocean passenger liner. This particular ship was destined for voyages back and forth across the equator, and subsequent reports noted that hot, salt-laced winds eventually wore varnish and paint off all the exposed wall areas except one — Matsuda's lacquered lounge doors.

In 1933 the 37-year-old Matsuda visited Europe, which was then in the turbulent throes of the rise of Nazi Germany. Upon learning of Matsuda's visit, Adolf Hitler requested a meeting with him. Matsuda recalls that the German dictator minced no words in asking him whether or not he had succeeded in synthesizing lacquer. Hitler's intentions were obvious: Japanese scholars were beginning to verify the principle structure and ingredients of lacquer — including urushiol, rubber and laccase. Lacquer had already proved itself far more durable than glass or porcelain, highly resistant to acid and alkali alike, with no chemical in existence capable of dissolving it. Hitler was apparently excited about the prospects of utilizing such a tenacious finish for military purposes, and when Matsuda announced that as yet no synthetic version of lacquer had been developed, the German clasped his hand tightly and urged him to press on toward success.

Now, half a century after Hitler's dream, a synthetic lacquer has yet to be perfected. But now in his 80s, Matsuda continues his dedicated work. He lives in Sugamo, a district near the center of Tokyo, in a house surrounded by bamboo, camellia, oak, maple and other foliage arranged as a traditional Japanese garden. Sparrows, kites and other birdlife find restful perches in the boughs of these trees, making visitors wonder if this really could be part of the loud, bustling metropolis. Next to his house is an earthen storehouse, ceiling and walls

There is no natural white in *urushi*, so Matsuda developed the art of using bits of eggshell in the lacquer.

Applying gold leaf from a bamboo cylinder.

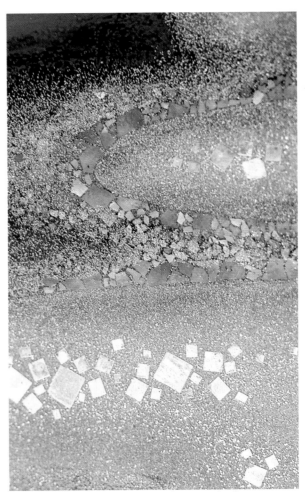

Mother-of-pearl and gold leaf are used to create intricate patterns.

reinforced with 30-centimeter thick layers of dirt and stucco.

Such storehouses are rarely found in big cities these days, but Gonroku Matsuda uses his as a joint study-reception room. Compared to the space in this room, the atelier in the main house is a mere cubbyhole — a two-mat room with a small, wooden-floored section attached. Matsuda has taken every precaution to protect this workshop from the outside environment: the ceiling is reinforced with a double board layer, matting has been laid over the wooden floor, and all sections bordering on the house have been closed off with double layers of glass and paper doors. Extreme care was taken to design a workshop which will not be disturbed, even by strong winds.

In the middle of the room is a low square table, 60 centimeters long on each side. On the right is a wall closet, on the left a small chest-of-drawers, and in the rear a large display cabinet — all within arm's reach. Matsuda explains this arrangement.

"I wasn't concerned with appearance when I designed my workshop — my only goal was efficiency. I've placed everything I need in front of me — there is no need to get up once I have begun. Why? For one reason, lacquer and dust do not mix."

The single worst enemy of the lacquerware craftsman is dust. Even the smallest fleck will draw lacquer toward it, causing spots on a surface to swell by as much as ten times. This means that

A Matsuda masterpiece: "Hinoki" platter.

Gold leaf decorates this ornamental table (height 27.5 centimeters, length 72.3 centimeters, width 38.3 centimeters).

work must be carried on without stirring up dust or allowing it near lacquer.

The reinforced walls are designed to keep out dust, as well as exterior noise. Extreme concentration and precision are demanded to create lacquerware which is pleasing to the eye at a distance for its composition, and up close for its fine design and patterns. The artist must truly become one with his craft, cutting himself off from all outside disturbances. A pendant-shaped light hangs down close to the surface of the work table, shedding the illumination which guides Matsuda in his delicate challenge.

Today on Matsuda's desk are a *natsume* tea box (used in the Japanese tea ceremony) awaiting only final lacquering, a small box containing mother-of-pearl, a bamboo stick with sharpened tip, and a tube containing lacquer — all the materials and tools needed for his most immediate project. Matsuda now turns his attention to his work.

Matsuda begins by placing mother-of-pearl. He has selected only the most beautiful, iridescent sections of abalone shells, having previously reduced them to small, finely sliced chips. He uses his finger to coat the surface of the tea box with a specially refined, transparent lacquer, containing a carefully measured iron content. Then wetting the tip of the bamboo stick with his tongue, Matsuda begins to place the mother-of-pearl, one piece at a time. Once the larger pieces of shell are in place, smaller chips are positioned between them to finish the work. After a breathless hour of non-stop work, a tiny yet exquisite river of shell flows elegantly across the surface of the tea box.

"I am a technician who relies solely on his hands," says Matsuda. He curves the thumb of his right hand outward to nearly a 90-degree angle from his index finger while working — vivid proof of rigorous physical training since childhood. When painting and coating the surfaces of rounded pieces such as trays, bowls and tea boxes like this one, Matsuda holds the piece to be worked on in his left hand, while using his right hand to direct his brushes in the rapid strokes required to create fine art. Resting a brush for an instant will cause individual strands to stick together, ruining the brush. To sustain the vital process, therefore, it is necessary that Matsuda's right thumb follow his brush lithely around the curved edge of the piece he works on.

Gold leaf gives this cherry tree design an extra dimension (height 7.6 centimeters, diameter 8.5 centimeters).

Urushi bowls bearing plum patterns (height 10.8 centimeters, diameter 12.8 centimeters).

"Crane" writing set.

The mysterious properties of *urushi* most fully exhibit their wonders in the art of gilding. Tiny bits of gold are applied to the lacquer surface in delicately shaded patterns. The tremendous adhesive quality of the lacquer makes this coming together of lacquer and gold a genuinely eternal bond.

Matsuda obtains his gold by special order. There are two types: rounded, coarser bits filed directly from gold nuggets, and much finer, powderlike gold. The gold is applied from a bamboo tube covered at its mouth with gauze. He first puts coarser gold into the tube, and holding it between his middle and index fingers like a brush, begins to gild the lid of the tea box. Once there is a thick coating of gold in the center of the lid, Matsuda turns to the finer gold, putting it into a tube formed from the shafts of swan or crane feathers, then gilding the surrounding area in the same basic fashion used with the larger bits. He speaks of this sophisticated process:

"By changing the slant of the gauze that covers the tube mouth you can adjust the flow of the gold. And you can alter the direction in which it comes out by changing the pressure of the middle, ring and little finger. The middle finger may push the tube strongly, or the little finger may be used to lift up lightly on its underside, much like stroking the chin of a kitten. When you change the angle of the surface to be gilded, the density of the gold overlay will also vary."

The decades of strict discipline have paid off; the tube moves as an extension of the fingers, spreading the gold into fine, intricate patterns.

Gonroku Matsuda — an artist who knows no limits when it comes to the pursuit of perfection in lacquer.

The 87-year-old master holds a *natsume* teabox, decorated with a view of Mt. Fuji seen through pine trees.

A Town of Craftsmen

Gonroku Matsuda, as both technician and artist, carries on the best traditions of the lacquerware craft. With his awesome creative instincts and dedication, he is leaving a tremendous selection of artistic examples for future generations to insure that the world of lacquer will remain an exciting and vital art.

Piercing an *urushi* tree to draw sap.

There are thousands upon thousands of unsung lacquer craftsmen in Japan, producing bowls, trays, cups and other implements used by the Japanese people in their daily lives. Many of these craftsmen have carried on the family traditions of past generations, always striving to create better "general ware." In a very real way, then, the sublime artistry of Gonroku Matsuda is supported by all these legions of dedicated "followers."

In the crook of the bow-like curve of Honshu, Japan's central island, is Noto Peninsula. At the northern edge of this jutting body of land is Wajima, a small town about 120 kilometers north of Kanazawa (the "little Kyoto" of the Hokuriku region) with mountainous terrain at its back and a clear view of the ocean before it. In the past Wajima was a gateway for the flow of culture from Eurasia, and over the decades lacquering thrust down deep roots in the region.

Tamotsu Kitahama, lacquerware woodworker inspired by the beauty of the grain.

One-third of Wajima's 33,000 residents are engaged in lacquerware production. The basis of the lacquerware industry, naturally, is the basic material involved – *urushi*. Approximately 50 tons of *urushi* are consumed annually in Wajima. Of this, about 47 tons are obtained from China. Because the domestic variety is higher in quality and collected in smaller amounts, the price is about four times that of its Chinese counterpart.

Wajima City started a strategic *urushi* forestation project about a decade ago, and at the present time about 75 hectares provide space for 75,000 trees. The primary conditions for *urushi* cultivation are a gentle climate, good exposure to the sun, rich land and excellent ventilation. This makes it impossible to raise large volumes of *urushi* trees in densely packed conditions – each tree must be planted at a set distance from its neighbors.

Kimio Kami (1929-) is Wajima's sole *urushi* forester. He picks out the trees to be worked on, and first opens a cut in their bark with a special

Yukio Kobashi, a lacquer undercoater for over half a century.

Kohei Furue, lacquer finisher who believes brushes are a major key to success.

Katsumi Komori, gilding artisan who feels the most important element is design.

Inlayer Shoichi Kokon: "The key is dedication, concentration."

scythe. A milky white sap flows out, and Kami scoops it up with a ladle into a bucket. The work is slow and painstaking, and Kami says that even on good days he is lucky to get about half a bucketload — or 800-900 grams. And even a ten-year-old tree will yield only about 120-130 grams of sap.

"The amount of sap in any given tree is extremely limited. The sap itself is a special 'medicine' generated by the tree in times of need — for example, to prevent deterioration when twigs or branches are chafed or broken in the wind and rainwater enters. The tree produces sap when it runs low, and you can only collect it once every four days or so."

Trees no longer yielding sap are felled, with replacements then nurtured for eight years before they are of any value. The *urushi* for which these trees are cultivated and then at last cut down is itself given a new life as lacquer.

Production of lacquerware may be broadly divided into three general categories: wood making, lacquering and decorating. There are artisans specializing in each of these areas.

Tamotsu Kitahama (1922-) is the current head of a long line of lacquerware wood makers. Specializing in wooden bowls, he works surrounded by the fragrance of fine wood — *keyaki* in particular. With tightly spaced annual rings and small pore-like openings into which the *urushi* seeps firmly, this wood lends itself well to the lacquering process.

After being felled, *keyaki* wood is dried naturally for two to three years, cut into lengths suited for the item to be created, then dried for another two to three months. Final drying is accomplished by smoking, burning the chips planed from *keyaki* lengths. This totally dried wood is not apt to warp. Excellent, well-prepared wood is the key to producing top-flight lacquerware. Kitahama withdraws a piece from his lathe, and lifts it in the air for examination. What he holds is an exquisite, flawless bowl, so thin and clear that the eye can see through to the other side.

"When I sense the wonder of the wood grain, smell its fragrance, touch its simple beauty, I am truly glad that I became a wood maker."

Yukio Kobashi (1919-) is a lacquer undercoater who has pursued his art for over half a century. The work of undercoating is the process which gives Wajima ware its great

Wajima lacquerware masterpiece portraying the four seasons.

durability. Between a month and a month and a half elapses from the time the wood piece is finished to when it is transferred into the hands of the artist who applies the final coat. During this time a total of ten processes are needed to insure an excellent, lasting undercoat. Kobashi speaks of his work:

"With the work I am doing now, it will take ten years to tell if it is truly superior or not. And when a flaw does appear, if I cannot distinguish the process at which it occurred, I have failed. While there are divisions of labor, someone who is not capable of all phases of the art cannot call himself a true Wajima craftsman."

Kohei Furue (1908-) is a lacquer finisher who began working at the age of 14, over 60 years ago. His garb includes a simple nylon shirt, designed to keep the dust down, and he says that in the past he used to wear only silk. While the materials of his art have changed over the years, the dedication and sensitivity are the same. The meticulously maintained wooden floor is one example of this approach; the fact that he rarely allows outsiders into his workshop is another.

The concept that a craftsman is only as good as his tools prevails in the lacquer world, too.

"The most vital tool in our work is the brush. Those used in Wajima ware must have hairs which are both strong and soft.

"Next comes the mixing of the lacquer. This is a substance with a particularly difficult disposition — it can't be handled like ordinary paint. The very same lacquer will change color between morning and evening, affected by temperature, humidity and other factors. This delicate personality causes us great agony at times. It also brings us great joy."

Precision wood working and lacquering are followed by the final finishing process — decoration. This is the stage which brings the beauty, the grace to Wajima ware.

The two most representative styles of Wajima ware decoration are gold inlay and gilding. The former involves inserting gold leaf into patterns sculpted with a special chisel.

Wajima's most renowned inlayer, Shoichi Kokon (1915-), notes: "There are about 300 inlayers and gilders in Wajima today, and the degree of skills they bring to their work is instantly identifiable. Craftsmen with lesser skills are quickly weeded out through a process of natural selection."

And it is this centuries-old winnowing process which has given "made in Wajima" its special cachet for quality, beauty and style.

CLOTHING

ORU
"To Weave"

A Nishijin worker hand-weaves a brocaded sash.

Silken Dreams

There is a saying that "Kyotoites are extravagant in their dress." This draws from the traditional excellence of Kyoto textiles and dyed goods. Representative of this art are the Yuzen process of kimono dyeing and the Nishijin sash brocade process.

Kyoto is surrounded on three sides by mountains, and the city is bisected by the Kamo River, flowing south — the only direction not blocked by hills. Said to have been modeled on a Chinese prototype, the shape of Kyoto as a city brings to mind a *go* (Japanese checkers) board. Streets run from east to west and north to south. Mt. Funaoka, from which the entire span of the Nishijin district may be seen, is a 100-meter hill at the northernmost point of the checker board. Gazing down from its summit over a small ocean of tile roofs which appear to overlap one another, small skylights are visible. These are to allow natural light into the workshops of weavers who make it their business to scrutinize closely the entire range of the color spectrum.

As the mecca of the Japanese silk fabric industry Nishijin's name has become synonymous with this quality and tradition. Annual value in Nishijin fabrics is over 260 billion yen, turned out by 22,000 power looms and 7,000 hand looms. About 70 percent of Nishijin silk is used to produce sashes, and the district ranks as a rare example of a large group of craftsmen in the same field working in harmony to produce the exact same end product.

Rows of houses with cramped entryways line a small, winding street. The steady sound of looms from beyond a flag-like curtain over a shop's doorway means that this is a weaver's home. If there is only quiet, then the shop may be a dyer, or a kimono crest pattern designer.

Fire extinguishers are too numerous to count. These tightly packed rows of old wooden houses are extremely vulnerable to fire. Furthermore, the high price of the silk fabrics being produced also makes it vital that every available precaution be taken against accidents which could result in conflagration.

Until the Meiji Restoration, Kyoto was the home of the Emperor and all of his household. And the history of Nishijin is as old as that of Kyoto itself. Over a thousand years ago a weaving shop was established in the area — one of several government-sponsored plants designed to turn out items needed by the aristocrats of the Heian Court, as well as officials of the government bureaucracy. After repeated ups and downs, Nishijin eventually developed into the cornerstone of Kyoto's weaving industry. This was about five centuries ago.

Today, interestingly enough, Nishijin artisans draw heavily from European technology. In 1871 three Nishijin craftsmen were selected to travel to Lyons, France. Their mission was to learn the latest developments in the silk fabric industry. Japan was only then beginning to emerge from over two centuries of near-total international seclusion, and traveling abroad to a destination as distant as Europe required a resignation that one might never return from the journey. One of these artisans, in fact, did not return, drowning on the return journey when the ship he had booked passage on sank. The remaining two succeeded in their mission, however, bringing back the knowledge of advanced European technology and of the renowned Jacquard Loom.

Sweeping mechanization followed, but the true greatness of Nishijin lies in the preservation of hand-working methods.

Even the leading weavers of Nishijin recognize the greatness of hand looms, and that there is absolutely no substitute for these machines when working on complicated fabrics or top-quality clothing. One of them says:

"In the first place, there is a big difference in the quality of sashes produced on hand looms and those produced on power looms. Not only do hand looms create sashes finer to the touch, but sashes easier to tie which will not loosen once in place."

Three years ago a particular maker introduced a computer in his operation, using it to produce the 20,000 crest patterns needed to create a single kimono. Working by hand, this task would require from one to two months. The computer cuts the process down to a single week. But this electronic streamlining has solved only one part of the time problem; doing other work totally by hand, it still takes up to a full year to complete certain types of sashes. The traditions of Nishijin continue to run deep.

Dyed silk threads — soon to be woven into a sash.

The home and workshop of a Nishijin sash maker.

Brocading is also used for tapestries.

A cherry blossom sash. About 70 percent of Nishijin work is for sashes.

Kako Moriguchi, an artist of the colorful Yuzen school.

Brocading is finished, and the kimono ready for completion.

Moriguchi's unique glue gilding technique.

Expressing concepts in a rough sketch.

New Life for an Old Beauty

A vitally important part of the Nishijin process is pre-dyeing — adding colors to threads and then weaving patterns with the dyed thread. The Yuzen method, meanwhile, is the exact opposite: weaving undyed thread into white, colorless cloth, and then dyeing to create another type of fabric with its own particular charm.

The clear, clean waters of the Kamo and Katsura Rivers flow through Kyoto, and up until the early 20th century the colorful sight of artisans engaged in *Yuzennagashi* (washing newly dyed cloth in the river water to remove the glue used in the process) was an everyday event. With today's concern for pollution of the natural environment, this process now takes place in man-made basins which circulate through the interiors of dyeing plants.

Yuzen is certainly one of the most advanced pattern-dyeing processes in terms of both quality and style. The school was established by Yuzensai Miyazaki in the mid-17th century, and it came to be known by his name. A painter of Japanese fans, Miyazaki succeeded in combining picture-like patterns with "glue-resistant dyeing." Glue placed in a cone-shaped tube is squeezed from the top, and applied around the perimeter of the pattern to be dyed. Pigment is then poured over the outlined area, and the entire pattern then covered with glue. The glue performs the same protective function as the wax used in the batik wax-resistant dyeing process, thereby preventing any effects on the subsequent fabric dyeing. It was believed especially effective in patterns of many colors.

Kako Moriguchi (1909-) is a dyer who has injected new life into this ancient tradition.

Moriguchi refused to be swayed by the accepted use of many colors in Yuzen and advocates the value of simple, bold, painting-like designs using no more than four or five hues. His reasoning is that neither a kimono nor its sash were complete until they were combined — two equal components forming a complete whole. Accordingly, it follows that the kimono itself should not stand out in an obtrusive or showy way.

"The first prerequisite is the appearance of the kimono when it is actually donned," says Moriguchi. His mind deals with Yuzen through images of the human body clad in its fabric. He is a fervent believer in practical, useful kimono, and seeks to return kimono trends, which have a tendency to drift into dimensions of the decorative, back to purer versions. But it took courage and dedication to take color away from Yuzen, because the superb technical skills necessary to create the colors were considered a hallmark of the process.

Kako Moriguchi was not born into a home with a long artistic tradition. He got his start, rather, as a live-in apprentice, who struggled to carve his own place as a master. He is a rarity in the ranks of Nishijin dyers, and was already 30 years old by the time he set up his own shop.

Moriguchi recalls many nights when he stayed up until the wee hours of morning. Eventually he arrived at the "glue gilding" technique, which heightens visual effect without increasing the number of colors used.

This technique involves applying a mixture of a thick glue, made of glutinous rice, rice bran, salt and granulated zinc, to bamboo bark, then allowing it to dry. Once dried, the substance is broken into fine bits, which are then positioned on fabric which has been moistened. This glue mix is classified into five categories according to particle size and is an adept means of shading wider areas of the fabric. It also allows creation of a third dimension by varying density of the substance applied. This breakthrough involves scattering the glue and then applying other colors by brush rather than bordering pigment with glue. It also allows the artist closer control over color sensation and tone.

The technique was a fresh wind to the world of Yuzen dyeing, which had been content to travel the same, proven road from ancient to modern times. Moriguchi is a master who believes that tradition shackled by form and convention is no tradition at all.

Two Moriguchi masterpieces: kimono designed to be combined with sashes to form complete, exquisite wholes.

Gekka Minakawa, a dyer in his 90s who shows no sign of slowing down.

Gion float; the "Chrysanthemum" and "Peacock" hangings of Minakawa attract special attention.

Beyond Kimono

One of the major events in Kyoto is the summer Gion Festival, a gala celebration dating from the ninth century. It is one of Japan's three greatest festivals, and its climax comes on July 17 with a spectacular parade of huge wooden floats decorated with swords, halberds and other paraphernalia, many reaching well over three stories into the air. Each one of the approximately 30 floats is decorated with samples from different dyeing and weaving schools and passes through Gion and then downtown to the delight of spirited, shouting crowds lining the streets six or eight deep. The parade is also a sort of "mobile gallery," which once each year shows off one side of the artistic splendor that typifies life in Kyoto.

A particularly eye-catching entry is the Kikusui Float of exquisite traditional design, which after being totally lost in a great fire of the 19th century, took a full century to replace. Now, with the immaculate beauty of a past age, the Kikusui Float is a prime example of the art of 20th century Kyoto dyers and weavers. It is also known more affectionately as the Gekka Float, after the man who dedicated 15 years of his life to its creation — Gekka Minakawa (1892-).

"Building the float was a real struggle, because of all the different conditions which had to be met. For example, everything on the cart must be able to stand up under the sweltering summer sun, it must be pleasing to the eye and leave a clear artistic impression when viewed from a specific distance, and it must be in line with the historical atmosphere of the Gion Festival itself."

Along each of its four sides hang traditional tapestries, woven with a timeless artistry. The themes of the tapestries are the "lion," "kirin" (a mythical dragon-horse), "good omen" and "peacock."

This development is rooted in the kimono making technology cultivated in Kyoto. Yet the road traveled by Gekka Minakawa differs from those of the majority of the local craftsmen. The son of a doctor, Minakawa declined to take over his father's practice, and at the age of 22 entered the world of dyeing design. While studying painting on the side he developed an obsession with things ancient, and moved boldly into research of vegetable-based dyes. The weaving techniques of ancient times aroused his imagination.

Minakawa says that his start as a dyer was at the age of 25, when the first small dyed item he had ever completed was chosen for display at an exhibition which, at that time, was the most famous of its kind. Although residing in Japan's mecca of dyeing, he had no real opportunity to grow accustomed to the disposition of the traditional Kyoto craftsman. He developed his skills and methodology entirely on his own, with his only teacher, safe to say, the actual woven products of past ages. With no senior masters to turn to for consultation, Minakawa's sole means of dispelling doubts and answering questions was to go to the library. Perhaps this is why he never felt limited by the definition or form of kimono, and in striving to expand the possibilities of a traditional technology pioneered an entirely new school of the kimono cottage industry.

Minakawa set his eye on wax as the resisting agent, not glue as in the Yuzen process, and worked to incorporate in his works a brand of beauty which had been almost totally forgotten from the eighth up to the beginning of the 20th century. There are still few dyers in Kyoto who use wax in their craft. Minakawa reminisces about the early days of his wax challenge:

"While glue gives a fine, distinct dyeing finish, in a sense it is just *too* beautiful. When I first began using wax the items I turned out appeared to be blurred, and it didn't gain much of a following. But after about ten years people began to appreciate the tranquil, gentle sense of the technique."

This sense, which draws from the delicate blurring and cracking which results only from wax, superbly offsets the elegant hues of natural dyeing materials which Minakawa dedicated his early years to perfecting.

Gekka Minakawa continues to create elegant folding screens, paintings and classical long-sleeved kimono. And, as a dedicated artist whose work on Gion floats brings color and joy to thousands, he stands out as a kimono maker who has carried his art far beyond the kimono.

A Minakawa creation: "Flowers and Birds of the Seasons."

"Long-tailed Cock" by Minakawa.

Yoshino Chiba, the living master of the indigo dyeing technique.

Picking indigo in the fields behind the Chiba household.

Newly budding indigo (right);
tennis-ball-size globs of the dye.

Hemp-making is winter work.

Three Women

"Japan Blue" or "Hiroshige Blue" refers to the dark blue or indigo hues used in the dyeing technique of the same name. In the days when farmers made up the great majority of the Japanese population, their work clothes were almost without exception indigo. In rural Japan the dyeing technique for such clothing was passed on steadily from mother to daughter, then from daughter to granddaughter — because it was the job of the women to make these clothes for their families.

This is somewhat different than the dyeing and weaving culture found in Kyoto. In their constant pursuit of elegant lines and refinement which would enhance the overall beauty of the finished product, the artists of Kyoto specialized, dividing the many phases of the process into separate art forms. Naturally, farmers could never approach such standards. Indigo dyeing for the common folk was distinguished by its simplicity and strength, with all materials gathered by the producer and all processes done by the immediate family circle.

Yoshino Chiba (1909-) is a living legacy of Japan's oldest indigo dyeing process. Residing in the town of Kurikoma, Miyagi Prefecture, in chilly northeast Japan, she is said to be the only indigo dyer using totally natural materials and methods. She succeeded her mother Ayano (who died in 1980), a designated living national treasure, and with her daughter Matsue and granddaughter Hisako (still in her 20s) makes up an island of the old female dyeing tradition in modern Japan.

In the fields behind the Chiba household's vegetable garden are rows of indigo plants — used for the dye itself, and hemp reeds — used to make the fabric. The indigo seeds are sown in May, then fertilized with the dung of chickens that the family raises. In August and September the new sprouts and leaves are harvested, dried in the sun and then rubbed. They are then stored in a loft, and with the arrival of the new year a special straw floor is prepared and the materials are moved along in a long and careful fermenting process. Around May 1, the time when this cold northern region at last senses the arrival of spring, a lump of indigo, about the size of a tennis ball, has been created. Then comes the process that endows this dyeing technique with its great uniqueness.

In May and June the indigo ferments naturally, changing into actual dye. Two wooden casks 75 centimeters in diameter and 150 centimeters deep are placed on the dirt floor of the workroom, with indigo and wood ash added, two parts to one. The ash must be obtained by burning oak charcoal on a large hibachi all day long. The lady master says there is absolutely no substitute for these materials or methods.

The mixture is then washed in lukewarm water, which is poured with extreme care. Matsue then slowly stirs the mixture in the cask. Two weeks will pass as Yoshino carefully observes the color changes triggered by the fermentation process. The dye is green at first, changing gradually to a blue hue due to the oxidation caused by contact with the air. Relying upon a sense gained from years of teamwork with her mother, Yoshino knows when the optimum color has been attained.

The year-long dyemaking process is over. Then the fabric made from the thread from home-grown hemp, woven on a hand-operated loom, is dyed in a mere 20 to 30 minutes. The labor of blending the dye seems like a dream.

The color of the finished product is a deep, pronounced blue. Yoshino Chiba's face is a picture of satisfaction. But this is not the expression one would expect from an artist who has just completed a major project. Rather, it seems more akin to the sense of liberation from the duty of finishing a single, assigned piece of work.

Yoshino turns to bow in prayer to the patron god of indigo, enshrined in an alter by a pillar on the dirt floor. Occupying a key position in this altar is a small *Kannon* (goddess of mercy) statue, whose face has been sculpted into a near-exact image of Yoshino's late mother.

"I consulted with my mother on every part of my work. Things always went so smoothly, and I was never afraid. Now it is up to me to carry on this tradition, and I worry so much that at times I can't sleep at night."

Faith, expressed in prayers to ancestors, supports the legacy of proven technology. This faith has been answered, and the proof is another year of artistic excellence.

Hemp thread awaits its turn on the loom.

Around and around on a spinning wheel.

Finished indigo cloth.

PAPER

SUKU
"To Make Paper, Filter"

Total Concentration

The Shosoin national archives in Nara houses many artifacts belonging to the Japanese Imperial Family during the seventh and eighth centuries. Among these priceless treasures is a family register used at that time. While silk fabrics and other woven materials of the same era are deteriorating with age, this paper register is still in perfect condition after 13 centuries. When the Japanese say that "Japanese paper lasts one thousand years," they are speaking more factually than they know.

Yet, even the Japanese themselves are beginning to forget the existence of this durable, beautiful material. Upon hearing that today the largest user of Japanese paper is the nation's Ministry of Finance, most Japanese shake their heads and wonder why. Why indeed. They don't realize that Japanese paper money, the most durable printed currency in the world, is made from this paper.

East of Kyoto is the town of Mino, the premiere papermaking center of Japan, where the craft has been practiced for 1,300 years. The Shosoin paper treasures were produced here.

Living and working in Mino is Kozo Furuta (1922-), a master of the paper-filtering process. Furuta is the latest in a long line of paper-makers, going back at least 12 generations and over 400 years in time.

"I make paper which will last forever. The methods remain the same — my father, grandfather and great-grandfather all produced paper in the same way as I do. When people ask me why my paper is 'eternal,' I can only answer 'it is because of the pure water.' It just happened that paper which can be made with the pure water of the area was paper which could last forever."

Like most of Japan's famous papermaking areas, Mino is surrounded by mountains, and has no land suitable for rice cultivation. But the fresh pure water of the Itadori River flows through the area.

Furuta built his home alongside the Itadori River, where he pursues his trade. The reason for the clear beauty of the river's water is the absence of dams or rice paddies on its upper reaches. Even more important is the absence of irrigated farms. The chemicals and fertilizers which would mix with the river if there were

Kozo Furuta, a picture of concentration as he creates his fine paper.

dams or paddies would shorten dramatically the life span of Mino paper. Paper produced with modern technology contains various chemical additives, and these ingredients actually break down the fiber of the paper, reducing its life span.

For each ton of fine Mino paper 100 tons of clear stream water are required. Unlike western-style paper, which is produced by processing entire lengths of timber into chips, Japanese paper contains only the bark of a few special trees. The materials then begin a long process using the water. First, after being stripped from the trunk, the bark is immersed in the Itadori River for several days to soften it and remove dirt. Impurities are then removed, and the substance is pounded and kneaded with a wooden club to carefully adjust fiber — all while submerged in water. Only when the paper is laid at a 45-degree angle on a drying board is it removed from Mino's fresh, pure water.

Straining Furuta's nerves above all else is the moment when he filters the new paper. The paper is mixed with a paste-like substance made from hibiscus. It is then scooped up with a filtering matt, and rocked back and forth and up and down like a ship dancing on a stormy sea. This is the heart of the filtering process.

This paper-filtering technology arrived originally from China. Then, about 1,000 years ago, a Kyoto craftsman devised the water-wash method, which led to a revolution in the paper industry. Japanese paper takes on its truly fine character only after passing through this process. The fibers of the paper substance being jostled on the matt are combined and strengthened much like the fibers of woven fabric. And when the paper is being dried, the hibiscus paste concentrates at the juncture of the fibers, creating a phenomenon which, in weaving terms, amounts to a coating over each individual thread strand. It is said that the quality of paper declines as oxidation occurs, but with this coating the oxygen in the air cannot penetrate through to the interior of the paper fiber.

During the Edo period it was simple common sense that paper must be highly resistant to water. When fires occurred, merchants would throw their valuable records into a well before they fled. Even if the building burned to the ground the papers in the well would survive, and once dried were as good as new. A tremendous

Newly cut bark floating in the Itadori River.

Elderly lady workers remove the dust and dirt.

The wet paper is hung on a board to dry naturally.

Dried paper is removed with great care.

range of applications was found for Japanese paper, such as rainguards, umbrellas, lunch boxes, and even armor and helmets. It is a material with great flexibility, comparable to the plastics of today.

Furuta notes that working for a full day he can produce enough paper to cover 200 sliding doors (a standard measure arrived at from the unified size of doors in Kyoto temples and shrines). Mino paper has been used for the doors in Katsura Imperial Villa, Kinkaku-ji Temple, Ginkaku-ji Temple and other national architectural treasures in the Kyoto area. Paper for this purpose requires rigid thickness tolerances, for if there was variation in the degree of light entering the interiors the entire look and feel of those famous structures would not be the same.

"All the homes of master Mino paper craftsmen face south. The most important condition during the filtering process is stable sunshine.

"We rely heavily on light in our trade. Orders come in specifying a certain paper 'thinness,' and we must turn out a varying number of sheets, all exactly the same. If for some reason strong sunlight were to touch the surface of the filtering matt, the paper will shine radiantly, and this will result in paper thinner than wanted. Too little light, on the other hand, will result in just the opposite effect — paper which is too thick. It is a matter of visual judgment."

Sunlight from the north is too weak, and with an east-to-west orientation the amount of light on the paper would vary from hour to hour. In short, the most reliable natural light shines from the south.

Sitting on the floor of a matted room, looking like a Zen monk, Furuta gives a scrupulous last inspection to each sheet of an order which will be sent off the next day. His fingers weigh the thickness of a sheet, and his eyes trace the grade of his latest work by holding it up to the light.

An eloquent linkage of water, light, eye, and hand. The result is exquisitely rare Japanese paper, now ready for hundreds of waiting uses.

Furuta uses his hands and eyes, and the southern light, to guide his work.

Dreams of a Papermaker

A certain famous Mino Japanese paper maker recently closed his factory, and in his final effort he used up all materials on hand to filter out 400 kilograms of paper. He had his last product delivered to Kyoko Ibe (1942-), who has earned the distinction of being Japan's premiere paper handicraft artist. Kyoko recalls her encounter with this master and the donor of the gift.

"It was about ten years ago, when I was just beginning to develop the concept of Japanese paper handicraft. He visited me after reading about one of my private exhibitions in a newspaper, and said he felt confident that I would discover new uses for this type of paper. We have kept in close contact ever since. Without the producer I would have no craft, and yet my work demands great understanding of paper-making. My orders are small in volume and difficult in nature, and they would not be profitable for any large-scale manufacturer. But our goal is to carry on the tradition of Japanese paper, at all costs."

Kyoko first developed her interest after seeing an exhibition of illuminated pieces by the Danish artist Kaare-Klint. Some of his most impressive creations were made from sheets of plastic, cut with notches and folded into cylindrical shapes. Kyoko flashed on the possibilities of making such pieces from Japanese paper, and with this sheerly accidental concept in mind, struck out on a new and original artistic challenge. After struggling to collect enough good Japanese paper she made a lampshade. Placed in a friend's living room, it drew an instant barrage of compliments. Experiencing the fine feel of the paper against the skin of her palm, Kyoko says she was overwhelmed by the inspiration to devote her life to bringing vibrant life and form to this material.

Kyoko's Japanese paper handicrafts are diverse. She makes lampshades, fans, shelves, tapestries, trays, letter holders, baskets, coasters, serving plates, bread baskets, tablecloths, covered containers, stationery, envelopes, greeting and post cards, fancy wrapping paper, necklaces, earrings, handbags and much more.

Kyoko is particularly interested in lampshade design – the area which inspired her to first try her hand at Japanese paper handicrafts.

Kyoko Ibe, Japanese paper craftswoman, in her workshop.

Paper tableware – returning traditional paper to everyday life.

"Japanese paper and light compliment each other. Light does not simply permeate the paper, it diffuses quite nicely. While it may seem that a naked lightbulb would be brighter, in fact a light enclosed by Japanese paper is more brilliant overall."

Kyoko does not let a concern for tradition limit her work in any way. She makes full use of the wonders of modern science. For example, chemical dyes are used to color individual sheets of paper, which are then arranged artistically on the frames of trays, coasters, baskets and other pieces using a chemical-base glue. Or, Japanese paper plates are finished with resin, making it possible to use them to serve food and to wash afterwards. Kyoko believes in pioneering.

This liberal approach stems not from her disregard of tradition, but from fears that tradition may die out altogether. There are serious doubts about the ability to continue production of this unique paper. All producers face the same problems: the advanced age of current masters and the difficulty in finding successors. A case in point is Kozo Furuta. With all of his sons having taken up other professions, Furuta's work will almost surely end with him.

What can be done to help the art of Japanese paper survive?

"The last resort will be to build papermaking robots. I definitely think it is possible to produce paper comparable to that of the great masters using the wonders of today's industrial technology."

Perhaps there are some who would call her methods destruction of tradition. But they could also be labeled an alternative means of passing on time-honored techniques to future generations. Talking with Kyoko Ibe, one is left with the feeling that the day when robots will filter and produce elegant Japanese paper is not necessarily very far off.

Paper shades soften glare while brightening the light.

Creativity and Consensus

As most Japanese art and many crafts draw their inspiration from nature, much that appears the same to the casual observer is actually different.

The nuances of, say, a simple piece of pottery are derived from subtle philosophical undertones which, by other Japanese artists, have been articulated in song and story. Deep meditation and intense concentration are common to all Japanese crafts for both creation and appreciation.

In the third chapter, we will attempt to delve into the inner aspects of Japanese creativity, which, over the centuries, has accomplished so much with so little.

Kaii Higashiyama: "Glowing Autumn"

An Artist's World: The sense of beauty is enhanced by all artistic elements being in their proper places in a highly disciplined form.

"I once felt sadness at the impermanence and constant change of all worldly things," the painter begins. "But I finally realized that there is not really anything sad in it at all. Impermanence is, rather, a manifestation of life itself. A flower perpetually in bloom would be devoid of beauty. The knowledge of the shortness of a flower's life, of its fate to soon wither and die, is what makes a flower beautiful."

The speaker is a man widely acclaimed as Japan's best landscape painter.

"Encounters with natural landscapes must always be considered once-and-forever affairs. Nature is alive, and constantly changing. The same is true of human beings. We are destined to follow an eternal cycle of growth and decline, life and death. Nature and human beings are forever linked to this cycle.

"If flowers and humans lived forever there would be no inspiration in encounters between the two. The brilliance of a flower's existence is manifested in the scattering of its petals. At the root of the sense of beauty felt while viewing a lovely flower is a subconscious joy of an encounter between flower and man, both of whom will exist for but a short time in this world. And this is certainly not limited to flowers; it holds equally true for the smallest blade of grass growing on a dusty road."

The painter is moved by the link between nature and humanity in the eternal cycle of natural change. It is in this common cycle that he identifies the origin of Japanese aesthetics.

His name is Kaii Higashiyama (1908-); he is a recipient of the Order of Cultural Merit, the highest honor awarded to artists in Japan, and famed for the superb murals in the new wing of the Imperial Palace where the Emperor customarily greets visiting foreign dignitaries.

After the more than sixty years since he lifted his first brush, Higashiyama still has vivid memories of his spiritual awakening as a boy.

"I was weak both in body and spirit as a child. I grew up in Kobe, but during my middle school years I spent time in the home of a certain acquaintance near the sea on Awaji

Island, close to Kobe. Day after day I would stand facing the sea, my back to the mountains, staring out over the waters. It was during these days that I first sensed the tremendous forces around and within my own existence. Nature, the origin of all life, gave me my initial artistic inspiration."

The sea at Awaji Island marked the start of a long spiritual and artistic journey for Higashiyama. As the journey grew longer it also came to cover more ground, as his studies led him out of Japan to Germany, Italy, France, Switzerland, England, Denmark, Sweden, Norway, Finland and China. And as he traveled, he sketched, taking full advantage of the once-and-forever encounters with nature around the world.

"I scrutinize the wonders of nature, and record these impressions on canvas. The reason I observe things so closely is not to analyze natural phenomena as such, but rather to understand the life therein in clear, accurate terms, without a trace of exaggeration."

The Japanese are moved by Higashiyama's work because within it they find an easy rapport with nature. While the locations depicted in the works are not specific, they allow the viewer to search through the lines of a symbolic landscape, and discover the joy of being alive. It gives a sense of plunging together with the painter into the depths of the natural world.

The Japanese preoccupation with nature manifests itself in interesting ways, such as the methods used to compose a normal letter. It remains common sense in Japan to begin a letter with a seasonal reference. This initiates a smooth entry into communications between two parties with a conscious reference to the fact that both are living in the same general natural environment.

But these seasonal references are not as simple as they might seem. While it is permissible to write "it is the height of spring" at the real peak of that season, when the first signs of summer arrive the writer must choose between "late spring" and "early summer." When a Japanese picks up a pen to begin a letter there is a moment of contemplation about the season of the year.

The age-old Japanese custom of sending out simple postcard-like greetings both at New Year's and at the height of summer continues to be practiced, and many Japanese also offer late summer greetings bearing reference to the "lingering heat."

An ancient Japanese poet once wrote:
Although my eyes do not tell me
That autumn has come,
The sound of the wind does.

The Japanese have never been content to rely upon only their eyes to trace the changing of the seasons, but instead use all five senses to the fullest.

In his close looks at the impermanence and constant change of nature and man, Higashiyama has been greatly influenced by the Japanese people's aesthetic appreciation for the cycle of the four seasons.

A comprehensive study of Higashiyama's art and of his decades of encounters with natural landscapes may be gleaned from examining a series of murals in Toshodai-ji Temple in Nara — a ten-year project which he began in 1971.

The Toshodai-ji was built over 1,200 years ago during the age of the Yamato Court (sixth to eighth century); it was established by Ganjin, a Buddhist priest from Tang China. At that time it was a brilliantly colored monastery in the gaudy fineness of the Tang tradition, which undoubtedly gained acclaim for its unrivaled splendor. Today, it is a picture of classic antiquity: faded colors and natural foliage have broken the rigid geometrical symmetry of the past, expressing a uniquely Japanese harmony between architecture and nature.

In the Miei-do, a pavilion located deep within the grounds of the Toshodai-ji, rests a stone statue of Ganjin. Basho, the prototypical Japanese haiku poet, composed the following verse after first gazing at this statue.

Fresh leaves of spring,
If only these drops of dew
Could cleanse your eyes

Higashiyama's masterpiece on the sliding doors of the Miei-do (Toshodai-ji). When the "Mountain Clouds" of the inner room and the "Sound of

The statue of Ganjin shows the priest with his eyes closed. During five ocean voyages and a dozen years of attempting to reach Japan and bring to the Japanese people the teachings of Buddha, recurring mishaps and hardships took their toll on Ganjin's eyesight, and by the time he finally arrived on the shores of Japan he was totally blind.

Higashiyama's mural was painted within the Miei-do. When he was first requested to create this work of art, he reflected on what images must have existed within the mind of Ganjin who, unable to view the landscape of Japan, was filled with ample memories of his native China. Higashiyama then decided to create a superb requiem for this famous Chinese priest.

Now, Higashiyama sets out on yet another journey in his endless search for the essence of the Japanese landscape. It is January. This time he is after the winter ocean, and heads for the frozen northern tip of Honshu, the nation's main island.

Arriving at a rustic station, Higashiyama is greeted only by falling snow. Gazing toward the Tsugaru Straits his eyes and soul overflow with a sense of the dark, freezing flow of the northern sea.

Traveling slowly south along the coast of the Japan Sea in January, Higashiyama arrives at Wajima City on Noto Peninsula, the midpoint of Honshu. Whitecaps dancing along the rugged coastline and the rush of the tide paint vivid arabesque images of the winter ocean. Neither blue nor green, the dominant color is the tran-

Waves" of the room in the foreground are all closed, they create two spectacular murals with a total length of over 80 meters.

quil, greenish-grey often found in Japanese painting, and Higashiyama senses an "encounter" taking form.

Only the painter is truly aware of the depth of this encounter. The Japanese coast is a study in variety. There are quiet, sandy beaches, rough, rocky shores, battles between fantastic twisted rocks and surging ocean, tranquil inland seas where sparkling spring sunshine reflects an infinity, and fierce raging tides of the open sea. The change in climate and configuration blesses the perimeter of Japan with a fathomless degree of fascination.

Once Higashiyama is rested from his journey along the shore, he turns inland to the waiting mountains.

For this trip, he heads into secluded areas by a primitive light railway — actually more of a tram. Once, there was even printed on the reverse side of the tickets a warning that the railway company was not responsible in the event of injury or death to passengers. The tracks wound their way through narrow gorges, on the brink of surging rapids and swift-flowing mountain streams.

It is the season of rich foliage and color, lasting from May through the summer months. Little by little, the snow and mist disappear, and the faces of mountains change expression. Higashiyama is once again awed by the infinite vicissitudes of the natural world, and strives to create the free-flowing lines of mountain mists and cloud formations.

He has written the following of his encounter with the Amo Pass in Gifu Prefecture.

"As I approached the mountain path, the rain suddenly let up and a mist rose over the valley. The path twists up toward the pass, and the string of near and faraway peaks between the valleys would be revealed from time to time, then be hidden again as I moved along. The infinite variety of shapes created by the mists clinging to the mountain surfaces, blending with light and dark green hues of the trees along the path, painted a fantastical, breathtaking landscape.

"This was a far more spectacular vista than ones which I had encountered on many journeys, and I drew upon it for the painting of the upper portion of the Miei-do mural. Standing at the pass, transfixed by the view there, I felt sure that someone or something had ordered me to paint this landscape. Usually when I stand engulfed in a natural scene which seems to whisper 'draw me, draw me,' I reach involuntarily for my sketchbook. But this time, rather than a whisper, I actually felt a voice reaching down to me from somewhere in the vast empty sky, telling me to take up the tools of my trade and paint this vision."

A painter guided by nature, Higashiyama has journeyed up and down the Japanese archipelago, and traveled to China to view the landscapes there immediately after diplomatic relations were restored.

The mural in the Miei-do of the Toshodai-ji is hard evidence of these treks.

This is not, however, a wall mural in the western sense. The images have been painted on sliding paper doors. These doors are thin partitions (*fusuma*) which divide a room into smaller sections, and are opened and closed constantly. This means that the artwork thereon must yield visual pleasure and significance in many different configurations — that is, with various sections opened, closed or overlapping. The mural, therefore, is a continuous flow, although divided into a number of rectangular door sizes. And it must encompass conflicting elements — tranquility and movement, the whole and individual components, even contradicting elements — before it truly takes on a lasting life of its own.

"Unlike in the West," the painter continues, "in Japan there is no attempt to present thorough, graphic illustrations of the many faces of nature. Stress is placed not on drawing or painting everything observed, but on what a particular scene actually represents in an artistic sense. Elements judged unnecessary are abbreviated or eliminated, with attempts made to present the essential contours of the object. While westerners seek to express cubic beauty in painting, Japanese strive to illuminate just how the shape of an object offsets the space in which it exists. This is why our linear sense is so very demanding."

Traditional Japanese rooms have tatami floor mats. When Japanese speak of a "six-mat room" they are referring to a room consisting of six of these rectangular mats, each about three feet wide and six feet long and fitted together like a well-formed geometric puzzle. In the tea ceremony, close scrutiny is given to the lines of the mats. Attention is paid to whether utensils used in the proceedings are placed inside or outside the mat edges, and with stitches visible on the mat surface certain implements are placed at a specified number of stitches from the edge. Rigid restrictions guide the ceremony participants. With the tatami viewed in terms of a huge sheet of graph paper, Japanese sense beauty only when all components are on their proper grids.

"In *Kabuki* or *Noh* theater, or in traditional Japanese dancing, there are strict requirements on the posture of the players. Human beings must be deftly incorporated into a clearly defined stage atmosphere. The simple purity that constitutes artistic beauty in Japan, therefore, extends far beyond the type of painting I do. It pervades almost every aspect of the Japanese culture."

A rich appreciation of nature sublimated by the linear controls of highly disciplined form — perhaps this is the ultimate core of Japanese aesthetics. Higashiyama lists the Katsura Imperial Villa in Kyoto as a classic example of this beauty.

Kaii Higashiyama reflecting in his garden.

Katsura Imperial Villa:
A structure never completed.
Additions are the rule,
with true beauty born in
the process of eternal change.

May 4, 1933. A German gentleman heads his black sedan toward the southwest through the checkerboard of Kyoto's streets. The sun is high, adding vividness to the red and black carp streamers swimming over the city's grey ocean of tiled roofs. Tomorrow is the Boy's Day Festival, and the traditional streamers looking like thousands of particolored wind socks herald the arrival of this important national holiday. As he crosses the old Katsura River bridge, the tightly packed wooden houses give way to rice paddies and quiet. The road continues along the west bank of the river, flanked by the timeless green of bamboo hedges. Finally, the man

Katsura Villa covered with snow. From right are the Old Shoin, Middle Shoin, Musical Instrument Room, and New Shoin.

brakes to a halt in front of an imposing gate formed from thick bamboo poles delicately interlaced with smaller branches from the same plant. He climbs slowly out of the car, his feet crunching the fine gravel that spreads as a natural carpet from the ancient gate — the entrance to the Katsura Imperial Villa.

Following his diminutive Japanese guide, he disappears into the awesome silence of this venerable place of legends.

They walk through the gate and step up into a hallway covered with soft tatami mat flooring, then through open doors onto the veranda.

Opening up before them is one of Japan's most beautifully manicured gardens.

Directly in front of him is a large pond, reflecting the variegated greens of the surrounding trees. In the center of this pool are two small islands. On the bank beyond them, guarded by the wild red blooms of rhododendrons, is the Shokin-tei Teahouse. The man swings his eyes to the left, where the thick forest growth stretches all the way down to the rocky shoreline. Here a white sandy beach glistens in the sunshine. This is Amano-Hashidate, said to be modeled after the area of the same name on the Japan Sea coast of Kyoto Prefecture — traditionally considered one of Japan's three greatest scenic wonders. Fenced from view by the forest are the inner and outer benches of the covered Waiting Booth, stage left and stage right for waiting players of the tea ceremony.

Next, he turns to the right. There he discovers a miniature archipelago, linked into a whole by three bridges. At the summit of a small man-made hill nearby is Shoka-tei Teahouse, and at the hill's foot is the Enrin-do Memorial Pavilion, its roof jutting up high above the surrounding trees. Further right from the balcony is a wide green lawn in front of the Shoi-ken Teahouse.

Next, the man turns his attention to the exterior of the building — the Old Shoin (main living quarters). To the right, stretching back as one wing is the Middle Shoin, Gakki-no-ma (Musical Instrument [Storage] Room) and the New Goten. To the left is the Geppa-ro Teahouse, and behind it are attached buildings including a more prosaic rice storehouse and retainers' quarters.

No paint sullies the wood, and only the finest natural materials have been used, creating an almost perfect harmony between nature and art; a subtle fusing together of a single flowing spatial existence.

A frog splashes into the pond from one of the islands, breaking the man's reverie, and punctuating his thought. Later, he was to record this moment in his diary, adding that "The beauty of the scene brought tears to my eyes."

The visitor was Bruno Taut (1880-1939), the eminent German architect who introduced Katsura Villa to an appreciative world. A Berliner, Taut is best known for his concept of "integrated architecture." He visited Katsura on his second day in Japan.

The veranda Taut stood on is known as the

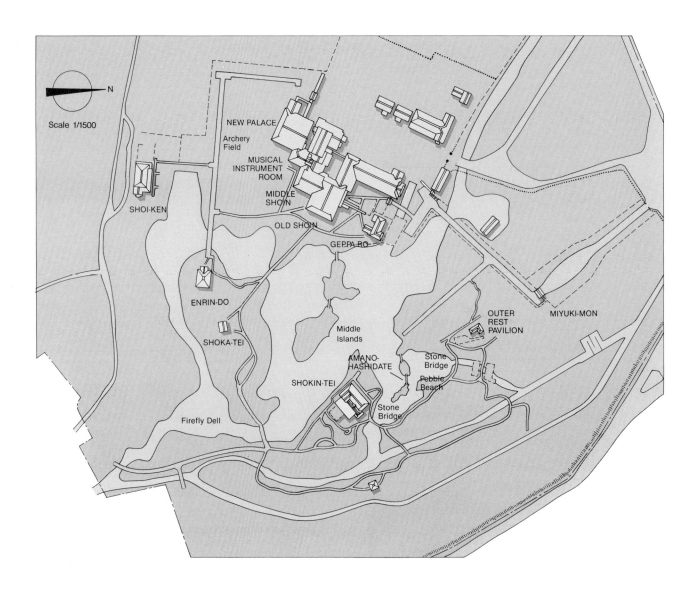

Scale 1/1500

NEW PALACE
Archery Field
MUSICAL INSTRUMENT ROOM
MIDDLE SHOIN
SHOI-KEN
OLD SHOIN
GEPPA-RO
ENRIN-DO
SHOKA-TEI
Middle Islands
AMANO-HASHIDATE
SHOKIN-TEI
Firefly Dell
Stone Bridge
OUTER REST PAVILION
MIYUKI-MON
Stone Bridge
Pebble Beach

Moon Viewing Estrade. Built from some 80 lengths of bamboo covering a chestnut wood frame, this veranda is four meters wide and 2.9 meters long.

Although it was early afternoon, when Taut learned that this was an estrade designed exclusively for moon viewing, his mind flashed to images of the garden at night, and he felt a deep thrill at the thought of the moon's reflection on the pond. This history of the veranda can be traced back to the early 17th century, when Prince Toshihito Hachijyo-no-Miya first set about building the villa complex.

The Japanese have always held a special reverence for the moon. The custom of celebrating the coming of the harvest moon (September's full moon) survives to this day, with rice dumplings presented as offerings and pampas grass used as festive decoration.

The space around the villa was carefully created for moon viewing, and the Moon Viewing Estrade itself was positioned with this sole purpose in mind. The platform is oriented 32 degrees to the south, which allows the moon to "enter" the garden from the far left, climb steadily to the right, and reach a pinnacle directly above the villa. Until just prior to its peak, the moonlight is lost in the tree groves, but as it arrives at its peak its full brightness is reflected on the pond. The sudden appearance of the light on the water is a breathtaking moment, and at this point the true genius of the garden's designer becomes clear. The trees stretching out before the viewing estrade were planted to orchestrate a tempo to the moon's movement and its reflection — a glimpse into a spiritual tradition which has attempted to draw natural beauty into every possible aspect of life.

Looking across the moon-viewing estrade of the Old Shoin to the pond.

Stone basin.

This sensation is clear from the first step into the villa grounds.

After ducking under the low-hanging gate to enter the complex, a dark gravel footpath stretches in a straight line for about 40 meters. There is a slightly raised paved strip running down the middle of the path to facilitate drainage, and moss and evergreen hedges flanking both sides heighten the the sense of linearity. The hedges, meanwhile, are very high, and block the view to the inner garden. Aristocrats of past ages were carried down this path in palanquins, and their view was obstructed as well. This visual oppression suddenly ends, however, as the path approaches the earthen bridge at the west edge. Standing on the rounded center of the bridge, to the left is a view of garden and pond even more impressive than from the veranda. This is the longest unobstructed vista anywhere in the entire villa grounds. To the right of the bridge is a berth, with a small boat tied to it. Visitors lingering on this bridge, inspired by the view of the garden, may feel the urge to board a boat and sail around the pond for a closer look.

Once over the bridge, the pathway turns to the left, and leads visitors toward the scenes described earlier. Moving further and further into the interior of the garden heightens the sense of anticipation. Once again, however, the frontal view is masked — this time by a single

pine tree on a promontory, which spreads its full branches directly into the line of vision.

At last, the path arrives at the entrance, and the mind is caught up by the creativity of the approachway itself. There are no walls or other structural contrivances — rather, the only elements are foliage, man-made hills and strategically placed natural touches. While the location of trees, water and other components may appear to be arbitrary, in fact there is an extremely intricate design. It might be labeled spatial aesthetics — the accenting of nature by nature — an art which continues to thrive in Japan today.

The arrangement creates specific impressions at specific places. The designers have actually given instructions where the eye should settle at each point of the path, and to assure this effect at times have blocked certain views or intentionally curved or sloped the path.

No doors, glass or other artificial means are used to partition the tea houses around the villa complex. The different structures are physically and visually separated by foliage and hills. Rather than struggling against natural forces, they have been adeptly utilized in a design which carves out individual pockets of privacy and solitude.

Bruno Taut was surely moved deeply by the powerful simplicity of the design.

Katsura Villa was built about 370 years ago as a retreat for the Imperial Family. It was used chiefly as a summer house and for moon viewings. A diary written by a Buddhist priest of the time records the garden parties held there. He writes about groups of aristocrats gathering at the different teahouses to drink tea and sake, sing and dance, and find other forms of amusement. There were also apparently excursions on covered boats around the pond during the merrymaking.

In short, the villa was not only a scenic garden, it was also a place for festive partying. The teahouses themselves were designed with this purpose in mind, to allow guests to fully enjoy themselves in a refreshing and inspirational natural setting.

Moving along the edge of the pond, the first structure seen is Shokin-tei Teahouse with its thatched gable roof. Bark-covered natural oak poles support the deeply thatched front eaves. Their wide spacing gives the teahouse the simple, rustic feeling of a rush-roofed seaside hut. In combination with the Amano-Hashidate bridge and sandy beach, the Shokin-tei conjures up ocean images. As mentioned previously, this Amano-Hashidate is a miniaturized version of one of Japan's three most famous scenic spots.

Strolling through the trees and coming suddenly upon this landscape triggers a feeling of the sea, even though all logic says that this is only a small pond. And arriving on this shore by boat offers an even stronger suggestion of a seaside. A distinctive feature of Japan's natural environment is climbing down from hills to arrive at the sea, and this sensation is present in the hills and shores of Katsura Villa.

At this point, a visitor may choose to step up into the Shokin-tei Teahouse. Inside there is a cool, shady atmosphere, created not only by the

Stone bridge.

Amano-Hashidate.

"ocean view" but also from the architecture: the structure faces north and has a miniature mountain to the south, so the teahouse opens onto the pond on the east, west and north — ideal conditions for enjoying the refreshing cool of a summer evening.

After relaxing briefly, a visitor can continue around the right side of the pond. A stone bridge is crossed to get to the large island, and the pathway then leads uphill to the Shoka-tei. Known as the "summit teahouse," the Shoka-tei stands on the highest point in the entire villa complex. In contrast to the seaside flavor of the Shokin-tei, this teahouse exudes the image of a rest stop somewhere deep in a forest.

The view is stupendous. Although there is now some interference from high-rise buildings, not so long ago this teahouse provided a sweeping vista of Kyoto, the old capital, from Mt. Higashi in the south to Mt. Arashi in the north.

The next stop is the interior of the Shoka-tei. Stepping onto the dirt floor of the teahouse, wipe off the sweat of summer heat and sit down to rest.

The Shoka-tei is simplicity itself. Again, the supports are natural bark-covered oak. Its width is 3.6 meters, and depth is 2.7 meters. The center of the floor is dirt, and with its west side open the interior is fully exposed to the elements. Other than the effort involved in drinking tea, a visitor is free to sit back and relax. The direct frontal view is tastefully masked with a cedar grove, and with low-hanging banners placed to further block the upper view of those seated within, the line of vision is forced even lower. This is to direct eyes to the grass, flowers and steppingstones alongside the path. The varying perspectives of the view from the Shoka-tei relax and still the mind — part of the overall plan of the villa's designers.

Shokin-tei as viewed from the middle island.

Interior of Shoka-tei.

Shoi-ken is a larger, rustic building at the southernmost corner of the villa. Only paper doors separate its interior from the outside world, and the south window opens on a sweeping view of farmers working in melon fields outside the grounds. While this is not part of the garden itself, it is certainly one more face of nature. In this case the goal is not to block, but draw a touch of the natural world into the teahouse itself.

The villa grounds were designed to allow visitors to enjoy themselves in a natural setting — playing games, drinking tea or sake, singing, dancing or reciting poetry. To achieve this, it was necessary to integrate buildings and nature.

It is an excellent setting for strolls, or cruises on the pond ending at one of the teahouses. These pavilions are designed to allow a visitor to pause and bask in a natural environment, before moving along to the next teahouse. This was the main activity of the long garden parties of that refined age.

When evening arrives, lanterns placed along the shore of the pond are lit. Fireflies flicker in the darkness, and the moon bathes the villa in its gentle light. Visitors would settle back, and contemplate the simple joy of being alive.

Stretching 200 meters from east to west and 300 meters from north to south, the six hectares of the Katsura Imperial Villa are crowded with natural beauties. Moving deeper and deeper into the trees, it is easy to lose one's direction, but this is solved by searching for the crest-like wooden carving of a mythological fish mounted high on the outer wall of the Old Shoin. This carving is visible from everywhere on the grounds and serves as a compass when moving through the garden's depths.

Pause for a moment at the edge of the pond, and gaze at the fish carving. The main Shoin buildings stretch off to the sides in an expansive, picturesque flow. Their straight architectural lines give them a feeling of a sturdy deep-rootedness.

Shoka-tei's thatched roof.

Entrance to the Shoi-ken.

After lawn football or archery contests and leisurely strolls around the teahouses, visitors would once again enter the Shoin buildings, to wash off the sweat of a busy afternoon.

There are bathing facilities in the New Goten: a nine-meter square, wooden-floor bath area flanked by a two-mat tatami changing room. With no bathtub, bathers scooped warm water from a barrel and poured it over themselves. The bathing area slants down on both sides, allowing the water to run down into slit drains. Pebble-filled holes are dug in the ground beneath the floor — a simple and admirably effective drainage system.

Off to the side are sleeping quarters, ideal for a quick doze or nap. These are the least-lighted rooms in the building, and while cool and refreshing are also an ideal place to keep warm in cooler weather. The floor is double-layered with rice husks packed between — a measure against humidity as well as cold. Rooms thus designed — elegantly simple yet functional — are found in various parts of the Shoin.

The Old Shoin, Middle Shoin, Musical Instrument Room and New Goten stretch back in overlaps. Each part of this wing offers direct views of the garden area, and all are arranged for ample lighting and ventilation. One advantage of this type of architectural arrangement is the elimination of connecting hallways.

While the villa was used primarily as a country retreat, it is a premiere case study in living comfort and durability. Its floor is set nearly two meters off the ground, with a wall area stretching down to cover this area. Some of the wall is white, in places made of mud and stucco, though most of it consists of bamboo hedges to screen out heat and humidity. This also reduced flood damage when the nearby Katsura River overflowed.

Beginning in 1976 all major buildings in the villa were taken apart, repaired, and reassembled during a six-year restoration project. The newly colored golden hue of the carved fish crest now shines like a beacon over the trees; the hushed majesty of Katsura Villa has been renewed and now blends even more harmoniously with its surroundings.

While the villa is a superbly integrated complex, neither the buildings nor the gardens were created at one time.

Prince Toshihito began the Katsura with the Old Shoin, and his son Toshitada added the Middle Shoin, Musical Instrument Room and the New Goten. Then for three centuries repairs and additions were continued to both expand and maintain the complex. It is clear, therefore, that the villa was not created overnight by the genius of any single architect. The gardens are the same, with plants and other features added gradually over the decades, over the centuries.

The elegance of Katsura Villa is the crystallization of dedicated efforts of unknown numbers of craftsmen and workers. Each new generation added its own touches to the buildings and gardens, taking care to preserve the existing beauty of the complex — a continuing architectural saga carried on carefully to protect and further nurture the highest forms of traditional excellence and flavor.

And this effort to create a lofty harmony between all three component parts — buildings, nature and man — continues within the walls of Katsura Villa today.

After viewing the villa, Bruno Taut wrote an essay entitled "An Eternal Thing: The Katsura Imperial Villa." In the traditional Western sense, eternal refers to something which never changes in shape or form. Perhaps the best example is the Pyramids, which have stood unchanged for thousands of years. Katsura Villa, in contrast, has survived for nearly four centuries while

Shokin-tei as seen through a window of the Geppa-ro.

Beyond the Geppa-ro's veranda an autumn mountainscape is visible.

The tatami and wood veranda follow the New Goten in an L-shape.

undergoing almost constant changes in structure and form. This approach may be seen in other forms of Japanese architecture as well — the philosophy that a structure is never complete. Ceremonies may be held to commemorate the end of construction, but additional building will be organized to meet any structural or functional demands which arise. There is no hesitation to adjust according to the purposes of use, and beauty itself finds its birth in this process of perpetual change. In change is eternity. A structure which never experiences change, whether it be after a day or after ten thousand years, will some day be ruins.

So, as an example of Japanese aesthetics, Katsura Imperial Villa remains alive as a calculated leap toward "eternity."

Sliding door finger catch.

Cedar door finger catch.

Sliding door finger catch.

Sliding door finger catch.

Flower-shaped cedar door finger catches. From the left are the flowers of spring, summer, autumn and winter.

Shoulder to shoulder —
from the foreground, the Old Shoin,
Middle Shoin and New Goten.

Gardens:
The calming influence of Japanese gardens makes them ideal for contemplation.

Landscape artist Kaii Higashiyama lives in Ichikawa City, just outside of Tokyo. The windows of his home open onto a spacious, abundantly variegated garden filled with white birches and other commonly found mountain trees which appear quite often in the work of this renowned master.

Although lacking classical splendor this miniature forest is a source of great peace to Higashiyama. From time to time he steps into the garden, surrounding himself with his trees. Stirred by a long lifetime of memorable journeys to different parts of the world, he examines each tree and shrub along the path with a sense of familiarity and deep satisfaction.

When designing this garden, Higashiyama laughs that he ignored the almost unanimous opinion of landscape gardeners who urged a formal approach. Instead he created a unique arrangement of natural trees scattered hither and yon — a garden he could truly claim as his own.

Many urban Japanese now live in mammoth apartment blocks. Deep down, however, most harbor a desire to live in a house with a spacious garden. Even those who are lucky enough to have their own homes and gardens complain that the garden is too small, and so seek through painstaking effort to create a garden larger than life and soothing to the soul.

Park acreage in Japanese cities is far less than in most Western urban areas. But Japanese make more of what they have, being able to stroll across even the most crowded park and gain some relief through a feeling of solitude, which, to the eyes of Westerners, does not exist at all. There nevertheless exists an almost universal desire for one's own garden, a piece of earth to reflect a particular aesthetic taste.

Surrounded by the sea and bisected by long mountain ranges, Japan is a study in variety, and one result is the popular recognition of certain sights and localities. Yet these famous locations have never been enough to satisfy city dwellers, who have traditionally wanted to recreate similar sights nearer where they live, so as to have access to beauty at will. For this reason Japanese gardens are never only gardens. Rather they are made up of a complex combination of natural "scenery" and "buildings." And it is this composite nature that has given Japanese gardens their uniqueness and made them an integral part of everyday life.

Situated between the interior of a traditional house and its garden is the *engawa,* a rather vague section which could be described as an "open veranda." While in one sense it is an extension of the inside floor, it is also clearly outside, exposed to the elements. This space certainly does not lend itself to simple definition. Although covered by eaves the lack of glass and walls place it physically in the midst of nature. The surface of the garden is "drawn" beneath log-supported eaves, thereby blending with the space beneath the roof of the dwelling. Only light and shade remain as the criteria by which to classify this space as "inside" or "outside." And while divided into the two separate dimensions of in and out, the *engawa* also serves to unite them.

To enter the garden, one steps down from the *engawa.* A row of stepping stones leads deeper into its midst, where ideally a sense of serenity will envelop the stroller. In the limited space can be found a rich variety of natural elements including stone paving, gravel, earth, stone, wood and earth bridges. While Japanese gardens are certainly not known for their vastness they are filled with man-made mountains and ponds, and trees and stones hauled in from natural environments in a calculated attempt to respond to the innate human drive to be one with nature.

When transplanting trees into a garden, traditional Japanese gardeners plan ahead, placing them with an eye toward several years later when the scars of moving have healed and the tree has become accustomed to its new soil. After the trees have been planted in their alloted spaces, a watch-and-wait game begins. Some trees wither and die. But the gardener extends no helping hand to these weaklings — they simply congratulate the healthier trees for their success. And within this process, they say, is

The *karesansui* **garden at Zuiho-in in Kyoto.**

manifested a truly natural birth. This is far removed from the symmetric, geometric patterns of European gardens which insist that plants obey the will of man. The Japanese approach is to leave the trees in their natural state, creating an environment which will bring peace and calm to the human heart.

At the opposite pole from this natural landscape garden is the *karesansui* (dry landscape) garden, another representative form of Japanese gardening which relies on symbolism. True to its name, gardens in this tradition are devoid of water, relying principally upon rocks and sand

for their beauty. They are not designed to facilitate amusement or strolls, but rather to be contemplated at a distance, from within a neighboring building.

Undoubtedly the most famous *karesansui* garden is that in Ryoan-ji Temple in Kyoto. It is surrounded by tile-roofed mud walls on the east, west and south, while the north side consists of a wooden veranda. On the flat, rectangular plot are fifteen stones of varying size, placed in five separate groups of five, two, three, two and three. They are set on a white gravel surface which is raked daily, the tines creating an infinity of fine parallel lines. While the typical *karesansui* garden contains no water, the Ryoan-ji stone garden goes even further, with no trace of hills, fields, valleys or foliage. In a strictly literal sense, it is nothing but a sandbox with some stones.

Moving along the wooden veranda, a visitor is compelled to contemplate the garden. Changing the angle of view alters the perspective, and the stone groups reveal countless combinations and faces. They have stirred the human imagination for centuries: Some viewers have said they see a family of tigers crossing an ocean, others see the stones as a scattered island chain, rocky coastlines battered by rough seas, or the rushing waters of a great river. The images shift,

according to the spirit and soul of the beholder, the light and shade of the different hours and seasons, and many other factors. It is clear that the rocks and white gravel have been placed with the express intention of allowing people to see what in fact is there for them and them alone.

A visitor selects a place on the veranda, and begins to study the stone garden. After a while, there comes a visual realization that the garden is not shut in, or restricted in any way by the short, stout wall on its other three sides. On the contrary, the varying shades of brown in this wall eloquently enhance the white hue of the garden's gravel.

Leaving this mind-moving garden of images and walking once again along the streets of

The famous circular grass garden at the Shisen-do in Kyoto.

Kyoto, passing through narrow entryways of many houses will lead to discovery of more and different gardens. Around a washbasin may be planted horsetail rushes, with small stone lanterns carefully positioned on the flanks. A garden of this type is a miniature of the gardens leading to traditional tea houses which have been copied by town dwellers and are themselves miniatures of a larger nature. In this small space often exists a powerful expression of the taste of the house owner.

Tranquility, joy, and deep contemplation are all equal parts of Japanese gardening which can reach deep into the spiritual core of the Japanese consciousness.

Stone garden viewed from the veranda at Ryoan-ji Temple in Kyoto.

Small garden paradises give the householder a place to relax.

Pavilions of Gold and Silver: Reflections of paradise in the transient world.

The Kinkaku-ji – originally completed in 1397.

At eight o'clock on the night of August 16th a fire starts burning on Mount Nyoigatake, Kyoto. As the flames spread, they take the form of the *kanji* (Chinese character) for "large." The character grows, eventually covering some 10,000 square meters. Other mountains with other *kanji* are now also alight. Known as *Daimonji* (literally, "large character") bonfire, this spectacular sight is an annual festival for the people of Kyoto — and through television for all of Japan.

Daimonji is part of the *Obon* (Japan's Festival of the Dead) season in Japan, when Japanese visit family graves to pray for the souls of ancestors. August 16th is the final day of *Obon,* with fires and lanterns being lit across Japan as signals to the souls of the departed.

At the foot of Mount Nyoigatake is Ginkaku-ji Temple, or the "Silver Pavilion," built five centuries ago by Yoshimasa Ashikaga (1435-90), the eighth Ashikaga *shogun* (generalissimo). It was from the Ginkaku-ji that Yoshimasa viewed the mountain bonfire in that faraway time.

A lover of the arts rather than war and government, Yoshimasa transferred the powers of *shogun* to his son Yoshihisa early in his life, then retired to the Silver Pavilion to live in seclusion. Yoshihisa, however, was a rather weak young man, and died soon thereafter at the age of 24. Yoshimasa was forlorn. Lamenting that the transfer of power was the cause of his son's death and wishing to offer condolences for the repose of his soul, with the coming of the next *Obon* season he ordered firewood placed in the shape of the *kanji* for "large" on the side of Mount Nyoigatake and then set it ablaze. Beneath the reddened August sky Ginkaku-ji today continues to cast a long, lonely shadow. And legend has it that the agonized cries of a broken father can

sometimes be heard from within the depths of this elegant structure.

The Silver Pavilion and the Gold Pavilion (Kinkaku-ji) are two of Japan's most widely beloved structures. Originally erected during the 14th and 15th centuries, both buildings are remnants of contemporary house architecture at the time, and both have superb gardens. The Gold Pavilion was built first, followed about 80 years later by the Silver Pavilion, which in many visible ways reflects the architecture of the former.

The three-story, gold-leaf-covered Gold Pavilion is a brilliant sight in any season, reflected elegantly in the large pond that opens up before it. In spring, backed by the fresh green of the surrounding trees, the pavilion is a place of sublime quiet; in early summer, with the pond covered with the snow of lotus blossoms, the structure seems to take on added strength; in fall, it becomes quiet once again, surrounded by the red and yellow hues of the season; and in winter, the structure stares down on the frozen pond in hushed majesty.

There was once a two-story structure known as the Tenkyokaku on the north side of the Gold Pavilion, and these two pond-side buildings

The Ginkaku-ji — an architectural jewel never "completed."

were connected on their second levels by a bridge. The view from that bridge, and the sense of walking through the sky itself, is still a subject of songs.

When Yoshimochi Shiba, a regional governor, visited the Gold Pavilion soon after its completion to talk with Yoshimitsu Ashikaga (1348-1408), the third Ashikaga *shogun* who masterminded the construction of the building, he is said to have noted that the beauty of the new pavilion surpassed even that of the Buddhist Elysian Fields.

The first two levels of the pavilion are based on traditional Japanese court architectural modes. The top story, however, exhibits a strong influence of the Chinese Zen school, and the pavilion delicately blends the aristocracy and Zen Buddhist tastes of the age. The lower floor was designed for guests, and has boat berths and fishing points adjacent to it. It is clear that Yoshimitsu used the pavilion and surrounding grounds almost purely for leisure.

The garden is huge, and offers different delights each season. It is a fine example of the landscape gardens of that age, which were meant for leisurely contemplation. This particular garden is also said to be a symbolization of the

3,000 realms traversed by Buddha, although it grew to be a place where visitors took leisurely strolls, or worked up a mild sweat in a game of lawn football.

The Buddha's ashes were said to have been enshrined on the pavilion's third level. Thus, presided over by the Buddha himself, nobles would gather to enjoy drinking parties, poetry recitals, traditional plays and other forms of amusement.

With a reputation of beauty beyond that of the Buddhist Elysian Fields, the Gold Pavilion was built in the exact image of Yoshimitsu's ideal. In erecting an elegant home deep in the mountains surrounded by the wonders of nature, and living there, Yoshimitsu wanted to taste paradise while living in the transient world of the present.

This same idea is found in the Silver Pavilion of Yoshimasa, although in quite different form. While the former structure was built to be spectacular, even gaudy to the eye, the Silver Pavilion, untrue to its name, is rustic, naturally colored — designed to blend into its natural surroundings in good Zen Buddhist tradition. The limited amount of paper used in the windows and doors reduced the amount of light drawn into the interior, enhancing the sense of almost religious austerity. While Yoshimasa did place a *Kannon* goddess of mercy in the upper level and held parties below, the gatherings were for tea ceremony, *Noh* drama and other high cultural pursuits.

In the Gold Pavilion Yoshimitsu sought to glorify the grandeur of this world, but Yoshimasa, a lover of the arts, was entranced by these images of the hereafter.

> If I could live longer,
> There is much more to learn
> From those around me,
> But my life has been that of the dew.

This was the poem recited by Yoshihisa on his deathbed. He dedicated it to his father. Yoshimasa's sorrowful reply was:

> This old fallen tree
> Should have rotted by now,
>   And yet the petals of a young flower
> Have scattered.

The "old fallen tree" viewed the *Daimonji* bonfire only once, then descended to the Elysian Fields where Yoshihisa waited. And with a silver-leaf finish never applied, the Silver Pavilion remained uncompleted forever and, as such, stands as a greater reflection of the original dream.

The "Daimonji" bonfire seen from the streets of Kyoto.

Noh:
Sadness is followed by happiness, then sadness again. Life is a wheel, turning forever in a chartable, circular course.

The lord of Ashiya in northern Kyushu is in the capital, Kyoto, on an extended visit. Three years have now passed and his wife is naturally worried, if not grief-stricken. One day Yugiri, one of her husband's maids, appears in Ashiya and assures her that her lord will return home by the end of the year. The lonely woman takes heart and starts counting the days until the promised return. One moonlit night she hears the pounding of cloth on a *kinuta* (fulling board) coming from nearby houses, and as if seduced by the sound, she and Yugiri also do the same. But the more she pounds the more her yearning leads her into a state of desperate fantasy. A second servant happens on the scene and breaks the news that her lord will not be arriving as promised. The lonely woman is totally broken, and certain that her husband has found more desirable company, falls ill and dies.

At last the husband returns to Ashiya. He is bereaved by his great loss, and taking up a bow, calls to the spirit of his wife. She appears, and tells a bitter story of her suffering in hell from lonely yearning and desperation, and expresses hatred toward her husband for his supposed unfaithfulness. But her husband chants the Lotus Sutra to put her soul to rest, and eventually she attains Buddhahood.

This is the outline of the famous *Noh* play "Kinuta," written by Zeami, acknowledged as the principal founder of that dramatic form. The impressive climax comes after the wife, face covered with a beautiful mask, dies in raving madness, and is then lifted up to Paradise as the sutra is chanted, while the audience feels relief at this denouement.

It is one form of *Noh* dancing and singing drama, formalized in the late 14th century, featuring a masked hero, unmasked characters

The classic *Noh* play *Kinuta* — the cloth pounding dance.

Kinuta — the dance after death.

off to the sides, accompanying musicians to the rear playing flutes, hand drums and other traditional instruments, and a chorus. The simple, abbreviated stage and plot lines are not easy to grasp for many Japanese, yet for centuries have carried viewers into dreamy, contemplative states. The deep, clear chants of the chorus caress the mind like a strange brand of lullaby; the masked actor glides back and forth over the stage with lithe grace. Slowly but surely, the audience is drawn into a world of fantasy as the conscious mind leaps into the symbolic unreal.

While nowadays mutual understanding of audience and cast allows troupes to abbreviate the long drawn-out plots of the plays, in days gone by *Noh* was customarily staged for an entire day — from sunrise to sundown. The stage was usually in a garden, facing south, and illuminated and shadowed only by natural light. Which plays were to be performed was determined by the movement of the sun: In the fresh light of morning plays featured gods; in the warm, invigorating light of the noon there were plays of men and women; in the declining light of late afternoon stories of derangement or madness were presented; and as the darkness of night fell upon the stage, tales of devils or demons took stage center.

Plays treating madness as above have traditionally been the most popular. *Noh* portrays madness as all-encompassing freedom, total serenity, and through the characters on stage the audience senses a longing for this "liberated" state.

Staged in tandem with the movement of the sun, traditional *Noh* concludes with a play about demons. The entire program ends, however, with a blessing for the continuation of plays the following day. Beginning again with a blessing from a god and concluding after dark with a demon attaining Buddhahood, *Noh* conjures up images of the eternal.

This is a clear reflection of the Buddhist view of the cycle of life and death: present life exists as a continuation of the past life, and after passing through the temporary stage that is death, moves on along into the next life. People in the audience gain satisfaction from this mood, and then return to their mundane lives with a renewed vigor.

Perfected in Japan's middle ages and generally regarded as a series of difficult riddles, *Noh* continues to be enjoyed by audiences today. Whether it be the inflections of the transmigration of the soul, the endless repetition of the impermanence of life, or other similar religious aspects, *Noh* offers a sympathetic and understanding statement on the human condition. Sadness will be followed by happiness, and then sadness again; pain will be followed by pleasure and then pain again. Life is a wheel, turning forever in a chartable, circular course.

Bonsai:
In the small individual universes of the Japanese people, these trees conjure images of a larger, often mystical dimension.

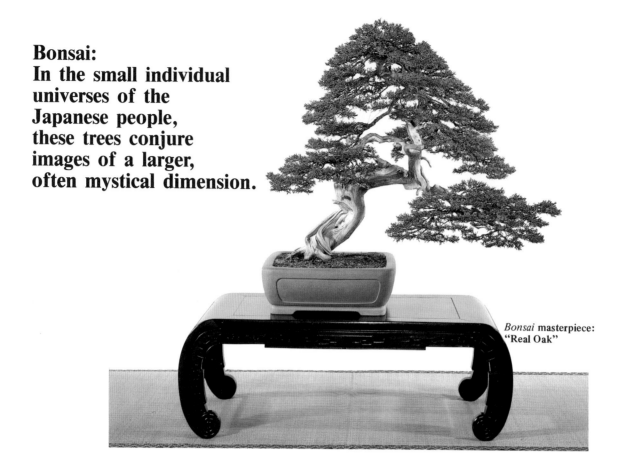

Bonsai **masterpiece:**
"Real Oak"

Lacquerware master Gonroku Matsuda has an avid appreciation of *Bonsai,* and is fond of sketching these dwarf trees, from which he says he draws ideas and inspiration for the designs of his finished pieces.

Most *Bonsai* are traditionally small enough to be lifted easily with both hands, pot and all. Pruning, trimming, pinching and wiring are used to stunt and reform their growth. The results are astounding: Azalea plants which after decades stand only 30 centimeters high; miniature pine and plum trees; and even apple and other fruit-bearing trees.

There is a long-standing drive among Japanese to reduce nature to a scale which can fit into the privacy of their homes. Perhaps the lacquer bowls resting on a table inside a house and the potted *Bonsai* sitting outside at the edge of a veranda are viewed in the same spiritual framework by the Japanese.

In a tiny garden *Bonsai* are lined neatly on carefully constructed shelves. Daily, at a set time the owner appears to tend to the shaping and watering of his trees. The satisfaction gained from these minutes is profound, and many *Bonsai* owners too buried in their daily work entrust their trees to accomplished gardeners. The owners will visit their trees on holidays or as time permits, discussing areas of particular interest with men who make their livelihood by understanding the fine points of the dwarf trees.

Bonsai lovers will often bring their favorite trees into their homes for closer enjoyment and to show to guests. They will also visit exhibitions and competitions to compare and to admire prize-winning *Bonsai,* and to gain ideas for future cultivation.

The care and study of these miniature trees is undoubtedly one of the most popular hobbies in Japan today. Chinese in origin, *Bonsai* gained a true foothold in Japan by the 14th century, and then strangely enough, proceeded to die out in its birthplace.

The nature we observe in *Bonsai* is not nature in its pure, fully liberated form — it is a nature cultivated under specific conditions, with color, shape and movement all given set qualities which reflect the "real nature" in passive moderation. Yet the question remains of what the Japanese actually enjoy in a "nature" condensed. One *Bonsai* craftsman has written the following which may shed some light on this query:

"Plum Image"

"Cultivated Cypress"

"For example, here we have a pine tree. Granted, it only stands a foot to a foot-and-a-half high. But take a closer look. Observe the way the exposed roots stretch and spread, the bend of the trunk, the extension of the limbs — other than sheer size, there is no difference between this tree and its huge cousin in natural forests. Now gaze closer. The branches stretch up toward the heavens, rising higher and higher until they seem to dance on the wind. The trunk bark has pealed away in an intricate, tortoise-shell pattern, conjuring up images of holy trees from ancient times hung with rotting lengths of sacred Shinto rope."

Bonsai lovers, like that craftsman, use the potted trees as a springboard to rise beyond realities of time and space. Huge, unfathomable dimensions are condensed, creating an easily accessible microcosmos complete with all elements present in the natural world.

There is great pleasure in the daily visits to water and prune *Bonsai* — communicating with these trees to lapse into imaginary, idealized landscapes. Furthermore, owning one's own trees eliminates the fear of disturbance or interruption. And for this very reason, the *Bonsai* and its owner share a common fate: The death of the latter in most cases signals the subsequent demise of the former. The death of the tree is usually attributed to changes in watering rather than pruning. Too much water rots the roots, too little dries out the tree. Only the owner truly understands the intimate particulars of this crucial balance.

And yet there are some very old *Bonsai* which have outlived several "owners." One of the most famous is a Japanese white pine first owned by Iemitsu Tokugawa, the third Tokugawa *shogun* in the 17th century. Although the center of its trunk is now totally hollow, it has been carefully nurtured for generations, and gazing at its gnarled form today, a sense of awe is felt at the forceful destiny that has allowed such a small piece of life to survive for so many centuries.

In philosophical terms, perhaps what the owners of *Bonsai* seek in the carefully pruned branches of their trees is, in fact, an escape from withering, a leap toward the eternal. In this regard, the most popular *Bonsai* trees are not deciduous flowering types, but rather, evergreen varieties. Nozomu Ikei (1923-), professor of sociology at Kobe Women's College, offers the following thought:

"Trees and plants which seasonally flower and shed their leaves force the observer to come to grips with the time-dominated realities and limitations of daily life."

In other words, human beings experience relief and tranquility in the presence of a natural life form which grows perpetually in the same steady, reliable form.

In the cramped space below the eaves of homes sit tiny potted attempts by *Bonsai* owners to defy what all logic dictates to be true, and to transcend the limitations of everyday life and death.

Living with Wood:
Finding one's place in nature means bringing elements of that nature into one's surroundings. In wood, the Japanese find joy.

Twilight is a magic time any season of the year. The warmth of spring and summer is particularly enjoyable, and the rapidly shrinking autumn sun and silent chill of winter evenings have their own particular charm. Visitors to Japan should take the time at least once during their stay to pass this mystical time in an old country temple, leaning against an aged pillar and watching the final vestiges of light vanish from the sky.

As the evening cool descends, the warmth of the afternoon sun continues to radiate from the depths of the old wood. In this warmth the Japanese sense a distinctive form of nostalgia — a subtle mix of bliss and melancholy and as good a representation as any of how appreciative they feel toward wood.

Living in houses made of wood and paper, straw-woven *tatami* matted floors, alcoves decorated with flower arrangements, and drinking soup from wooden bowls and using wooden chopsticks, the Japanese have always placed high value on wood as the most plentiful natural resource available for creating their homes. In the course of centuries they have learned to love the substance of wood as a dear friend.

In ancient times the Japanese firmly believed that the vegetation around them contained spirits, and that Gods descended to earth through trees. The forest stretching out behind a dwelling was thought to be the abode of the local Gods, and such woods could be depended on to protect the family living there from misfortune or calamity.

A lush green forest stretches up from the banks of the crystal clear Isuzu River in Mie Prefecture. Deep in this glade, surrounded on all sides by the essence of nature, is Ise Shrine, a simple thatch-roofed, plain wooden structure,

The fresh green of a bamboo grove.

recognized as the most holy Shinto shrine for centuries. The untouched landscape and virgin forest surrounding it are a dramatic example of the best in classical Japanese aesthetic tastes, whose origins reach back far before the arrival of Buddhism.

The experience of standing before this plain wood shrine and listening to the echo of the two hands clapping in a gesture of prayer to the Gods within, stirs much the same emotions in the heart of a Japanese today as it did centuries ago: The simple joy of standing in the woods, of being at one with nature, and with the Gods.

Ever since its erection in the seventh century, Ise Shrine has been rebuilt every 20 years. The structure is dismantled, leaving only the stone foundation. The old wood is burned in a sacred ceremony, and the shrine totally rebuilt to the exact dimensions as before using new wood. The first rebuilding took place in 690; the most recent in 1973.

It is said that in the ancient court, the Emperor would never use the same comb for more than one day. But the practice was obviously not limited to the Emperor's comb because excavations have unearthed a huge number of barely used chopsticks, tableware and other wooden utensils all over the old capital, remnants of an almost fanatical demand for purity in wood at that time. Though this has largely died out today, many families still faithfully repaper their *shoji* doors or put in new *tatami* matting at the end of each year to launch the new one in a fresh, renewed spirit.

Yoshio Akioka, professor at Kyoritsu Women's University in Tokyo, has explained this phenomenon:

"I believe the Japanese pursuit of culture is deeply rooted in the sense of touch — a culture of touching with the hands, the skin. Good examples still very applicable today include feeling of bare feet on *tatami,* or touching the sides of a *hinoki* wood bathtub while bathing. And most homes continue to give dinner guests new wooden chopsticks to eat with. These throwaway utensils have a nice feeling against the skin and are light and easy to use."

Rising from the surface of plain wood is a sense of softness, warmth, and a faint, fragrant odor. The sweet smell of a *hinoki* bath cleanses body and soul, too — plain wood is a great stimulant to the olfactory sense as well.

Rows of tall cedar in the northern mountains.

Jiro Kohara, professor at Chiba Institute of Technology and an accomplished scholar in the study of the physical properties of wood, notes:

"When purchasing a house or furniture it is natural to select things made of wood or cotton. Having once lived and breathed themselves, these materials are most effective in bringing a sense of ease and peace to humans, who themselves are also living beings."

If actions are indicative of beliefs, then the Japanese certainly fit this theory. While today wood is being replaced in architecture and interior design with concrete, aluminum, plastic and other synthetic materials, the Japanese continue to seek the "feeling" of wood by stenciling wood patterns on plastic chopsticks, aluminum sashes, and so forth. And within the cold confines of streamlined modern concrete buildings can be found no shortage of traditional-style Japanese eating and drinking establishments whose interiors are built entirely from natural materials. This is evidence of the persistent Japanese effort to, in some way and some form, retain the appearance and touch and fragrance of wood.

The Japanese love of wood runs deep. And it is impossible to discuss Japan without giving ample consideration to the love of nature and wood, the most plentiful and versatile material for man.

Grandeur in wood — Ise Shrine.

Quality Through Harmony

Will Japan's tradition of creative craftsmanship survive this century?

Hopefully it will, with the legacy of past diligence alive and well in Japanese factories, laboratories and executive offices today. To most Japanese, quality has an almost religious significance and the attitudes of craftsmanship are protected at all costs.

In our final chapter, we will look at the new generation of Japanese "craftsmen," who if not using the same tools as their predecessors certainly do share the same commitment to quality, attention to detail, self-discipline and cooperation with their fellow men.

In our first three chapters we examined the modern masters of Japan's traditional arts, and how and why time still honors their work.

Traditions which began many centuries ago remain a vital part of Japan's cultural consciousness, more deeply embedded in hearts and minds than even most Japanese themselves realize.

Limited arable land, a geography hostile to easy overland communication, the regularity of the seasons and a dearth of natural resources have all contributed to the formation of Japan's unique cultural traditions and lifestyle. The Japanese people use the limited amount of living space available to its ultimate capacity. They add more comfort, pleasure and quality to limited space. In other words, they make it completely harmonious with nature. This can also be seen in a preference for tools and implements used for daily life excelling in both aesthetic form and practical function, which has been passed on from generation to generation.

Over the centuries, craftsmen have pushed themselves to respond to the needs and desires of their fellow citizens by placing their work in a larger cultural context. And these craftsmen, with their unique cultural tradition, have also immersed themselves in the ideal of functional beauty.

In their products they aim for an ultimate harmony of quality, beauty and practicality. This goal is not simply to satisfy as many people as possible, but rather, to express in a finished ware their own ideals. To achieve artistic harmony is to reflect the mind and soul of the artist in a finished work. Such masters never allow a creation they are not totally satisfied with to leave their workshops. This spiritual stoicism gives precedence to personal character and a professional etiquette rather than purely manual skills when training successors. This concept is rooted in the belief that technique concerned only with the working itself will never yield truly exceptional results. Human as well as technical qualities are given extraordinary value. Lacquerware master Gonroku Matsuda has put it this way.

"If the crucial human qualities are not present only technique will advance and the result will be a distortion of what should be."

Japan's three centuries of virtual seclusion from the rest of the world during the Tokugawa *shogunate* kept the nation ignorant of the industrial revolution reshaping the West. When the nation finally and somewhat reluctantly reopened its doors, it found itself generations behind much of the rest of the world. The fact that in the next century she would pull herself equal in technology to the most advanced countries of Europe and America is one of history's more interesting sagas.

Terms like "diligence," "innate conservatism," "homogeneity," "wholeness," "harmony" and "respect for excellence" are bandied about by experts as explanations of that cliche, the Japanese "economic miracle." Others, however, see Japan's tradition of craftsmanship as the key to industrial success.

But to say this invites seemingly unreconcilable contradiction. Japan's economic strength today is a direct result of highly rationalized mass production; the exact opposite seemingly of the painstaking manual work of the traditional arts and crafts.

Can the two be linked in some way?

To see if such a link exists, we visited a number of Japan's most modern factories to talk with both management and line workers. And what we found seemed to support this contention in many ways. As a case study, we took a close look at the product which today symbolizes Japanese technology as much as silk did a century ago: the automobile.

Some have said that automobiles are accurate reflections of the nations which build them. This may be true if stereotypes are any indication: German cars are solid and mechanically reliable; English ones are traditional and formal; their Italian counterparts are stylish; French ones are sophisticated and unique; and American cars are very special in their own particular way.

This is an oversimplification, of course. Since domestic users normally account for by far the highest proportion of sales, it is only natural that a car be built to reflect their needs and desires. And it is here that all of Japan's limitations have become a happy accident for Japanese car makers.

As we pointed out earlier, Japan is a long, narrow strip of land, stretching more than 3,000 kilometers north to south, and embracing almost every known climatic extreme and geographic feature. As result, cars built for Japan must be able to stand up to the minus-30-degree-centigrade winters of Hokkaido; scorching summers of plus 40 degrees centigrade in the plains of Honshu; withstand downpours of 100mm of rain in an hour; traverse snowy mountains; and survive corrosive coastal winds.

There are ten Japanese cities with populations of more than one million and 44 of more than 300,000. Traffic jams, needless to say, are common. The nation has over 3,500km of expressways; yet thousands of kilometers of rural roads remain, some of which are still no

more than dirt paths. In fact, less than half of all road mileage is paved at all. Furthermore, natural resources and energy are quite limited.

In other words, when designing a car for Japan, the result is a vehicle which can cope with the multitude of different conditions found elsewhere in the world.

Shinichiro Sakurai (1929-) of Nissan, widely recognized as one of Japan's foremost automotive designers, notes:

"Automobiles appeal to the eye for their structural beauty and luxury, and to all five senses for their driving function out on the road. Both areas are crucial, and it goes without saying that they must be harmonized. If forced to choose, however, I would have to say that the suspension, brakes and wheels are the most vital components in an auto. It is my personal creed that even with the most powerful engine made any car is only as good as these three areas, because they are the primary factors governing driving ease, safety and comfort in all types of weather and under all sorts of driving conditions. And the types of roads found in Japan make it necessary to channel especially keen efforts into the design of the suspension."

Or, as earlier craftsmen have repeatedly said: the tool must harmonize with its wielder.

The traditional Japanese concern with fine detail has also paid considerable dividends to modern Japanese industry.

Minoru Tanaka (1930-), a designer of a number of top-selling Japanese automobiles, explains:

"The ultimate quality of Japanese cars can be seen upon close examination. The great majority of Japanese are very adept with their hands, and such people demand a superlative finish in any product that they buy.

"Perhaps this is also a reflection of the Japanese people's intimate familiarity with the 'art' of their daily tools and utensils. Whatever the reason, I do know for a fact that almost all customers minutely scrutinize an automobile before they decide to purchase."

In one way this has complicated the role of the designer. Purchasers inspect a paint job keeping in mind the fine *urushi* lacquer finish most have experienced firsthand with soup bowls and common kitchen utensils. It has been said that foreigners are surprised that Japanese seldom let their cars become dirty — an effort of some significance when one considers the heavy rainfall here — but this is part of a larger ethic. Japanese look at their cars as an extension of their living space and would no more tolerate a dirty car than they would a dirty home.

Tanaka also sees a similar relationship between car design and the carefully fitted components of Japanese architecture, where the slightest misalignment of, say, the papered doors, can destroy the carefully balanced sense of space and tranquility found in average Japanese homes.

"Many Japanese are very strict about the fit of things, be it the lid to a box or the swing of a door. If a car designer does not consider this crucial area at the earliest stages of his effort, nothing can be done on the production line to correct it. We call this 'designing-in quality.' It is interesting to note that a Japanese will think a particular car is 'defective' if there is even a minute gap where none should exist or a non-uniform gap where one should. This is why they examine the fitting of doors and hoods so carefully. It is part of a national subconsciousness that a good fit means good quality."

One of Tanaka's young colleagues on the Nissan design team echoes his thoughts:

"On one hand we strive to develop the most technologically advanced automobiles possible, but on the other we are also drivers ourselves who know and respect what our fellow non-engineer drivers are looking for in a car. I personally feel that 'touch' is the key to any successful car design, apart from any technological consideration.

"By 'touch' I mean everything from the feel of the steering wheel and seat to the absences of any large areas of uncovered metal which, in contrast to wood especially, would give a 'cold' touch to a car's interior. There are many other factors which we must consider, and these we have come to group under the very broad heading of 'sense engineering.'"

Sakurai, the master of the automobile art, puts it in a slightly different way:

"We are moving out of the age where good looks and good reliability are the keys to a car's success. People are looking more into the basic essence of a car — as in the past when they have looked for essence as the result of a craft. Today, the customer is looking more at what is in the car, and this 'what' is now advanced technology. We must nevertheless guard against our instincts as engineers to go too far afield. Any technological improvement must actually improve the car's characteristics from the driver's viewpoint. We must never merely accept new technology for the sake of technology alone. Japanese craftsmanship has always stressed superb applicability arising from excellent fabrication techniques, and we auto designers must always consider ourselves craftsmen of the highest degree."

Three men and three different ideas: Sakurai with a call for function; Tanaka with an accent on the fine finish; and the representative of the new generation of designers who sees a need for "touch." All three, however, share the same preoccupations of their predecessors toward quality fulfillment and exactness of purpose.

Lacquerware master Gonroku Matsuda notes:

"My teachers are the artists of past ages, who have left behind superb examples to follow. I am continually moved by what they accomplished. This feeling stems, not so much from the excellent detail and accuracy of their workmanship, as from their refined grace. They are clear reflections of the artists who created them. In other words, I find more value in the humanity present than in the technical expertise. If sheer technique outruns all else, true refinement will not be achieved. In the old days one would have to become an apprentice in order to receive the teaching of a master. This was viewed as a form of artistic etiquette, and a means of teaching discipline and weeding out those lacking in character."

Matsuda's gold and silver lacquer techniques have received great praise for their consummate balance of two key aesthetic components — intricate design and elegant *urushi* finish. The labor involved is itself more demanding in detail and physical endurance than an ordinary man could ever conceive. This is an art which demands more than just technical excellence. Without sublime spiritual strength enhancing each piece of work with clear, personal expression, even the most superb technique will never blossom into true refinement, true art.

This spiritual aspect is also recognized by Kazuo Inamori, the youthful president of one of Japan's fastest growing companies, Kyocera Corporation:

"Modern management techniques tend to thrust aside all bothersome human and philosophical concerns, and concentrate instead on clear-cut rationalistic solutions to all problems. But a product created by only the rational approach will create little if any impression on the person who eventually uses it."

Takashi Wakabayashi (1936-), manager of Nissan's International Vocational Training Competition (IVTC) and rally racing teams, agrees:

"In both the IVTC and rally racing the final determinant of victory is purely a human thing. You must balance the sides of your character. I have noticed if people cultivate their spiritual and intellectual sides simultaneously, something really inspirational happens — and these are the people I usually meet at the winners' circle."

Wakabayashi's ideas seem to work, too, as revealed by the winner of the 1981 IVTC:

"Manager Wakabayashi is an intimidating person. He bawled me out many times. He was very exacting, and everything he said had to do with etiquette — he told us to study the technical side on our own. I felt like telling him to lay off many times, but when I won the championship the thing that made me happiest was that Manager Wakabayashi was just as happy. I finally understood why so much stress had been put on etiquette, and that it was the major spiritual factor in my victory in that it allowed me to compete in an utterly calm frame of mind, as if I had been practicing for years."

To Japanese managers — and Japanese craftsmen — "attitude" is the most important intangible of quality.

Improving production technology and heightening productivity — both of these challenges demand good equipment and machines, but to an equal degree they need excellent relations between labor and management and a superbly trained work force. The latter factor has close ties with workmanship. Every company has its own environment, its own culture. So, naturally, there are subtle differences in the workmanship at each firm. To learn more about the similarities we visited a Nissan factory. The particular facility we toured is 97 percent automated, and has some of the most advanced production equipment to be found in the Japanese auto industry. Our central theme in analyzing this plant was, more than any other area, the position of workers who are in competition with this high degree of automation.

The first person we spoke to was the plant manager, who helped put the whole question of automation into perspective for us:

"We believe strongly that workers are our most important asset. We and they have both invested considerable time in training. It is certainly true that one of our primary goals is high productivity and quality through automation of the production process. To attain this goal, we feel it is necessary to withdraw human beings from work that is dangerous, puts an excessive demand on workers, is bad for the health, repetitive or just downright boring. We would much rather have machines do such tasks, so workers can engage in more rewarding work."

Examples of this philosophy abounded in the plant. For example, for 800 automobiles to roll off the assembly line in a day, a single human worker would have to wield a 50 kilogram unit to spot weld at more than 30,000 points. This, in many ways, is mindless work. It is also dangerous and exhausting. Removing people from such jobs also tends to improve quality.

The few human workers at the plant instead take care of the robots, extremely complex pieces of machinery. To them, their particular robots are extremely sophisticated tools with which to work a modern craft, and they respect them as much as earlier artisans did their chisels and brushes. The man-tool communication here is so intimate, in fact, that each robot has been given a nickname by its master.

The attitude of the workers there is amazingly reminiscent of the older generation, as witnessed by the remarks of one young line supervisor:

"I don't really know who will be driving this car eventually, or what its ultimate use will be. But I do know one thing: I don't want its owner to ever have a problem and wonder who failed in his job. I feel the same way about every car that comes off my line; it has to be perfect in all respects."

His sentiments were echoed by every worker we spoke with, and the craftsman-like dedication to quality work was apparent in every aspect of the factory's operation.

Management actively cultivates this attitude and provides plenty of opportunities for workers at all levels to advance as far as their talents and desires will take them.

Mass production is no more a barrier to craftsmanship than the substitution for wood of gas or electricity to fire a kiln. And a craftsman was no less of one if he used non-skilled workers in another age to carry his water and clay.

It would appear that the situation at Nissan is repeated elsewhere. In many industries there is wide use of numerically controlled machinery and robots. Insofar as this equipment is stimulating improvement in production technology and boosting productivity in a very tangible way, it represents a major contribution to corporate management. Moreover, there has been no reduction of employment opportunities as a result. Whether this situation can be maintained is yet another question, and one which conjures up no shortage of misgivings. At Nissan, however, an agreement exists between management and labor that consensus will be reached before promoting further automation.

So, despite the fact that new tools and new processes are being used, the results are quite similar. And that all-important question of attitude, of maintaining harmony with the different aspects of creation, remains alive in the hearts and minds of the Japanese as designers, builders, technicians, managers and consumers.

There is no guarantee that this attitude toward quality through harmony will not become diluted in the decades and centuries to come. But from what we have seen of the living yesterdays and tomorrows of Japanese craftsmanship, we believe that modern science and traditional values can and will coexist as our world continues to search for a better life for all.

"Quality" of automobiles today refers to more than just good finish, a nice interior and solid performance. Many other demands must be fulfilled to meet today's social requirements, such as extended durability, economical operation, low pollution levels and improved safety.

"Quality" goes far beyond makers boosting productivity and production technology. Every effort must be made to respond to the needs of society and satisfy the wants of consumers. This means that topflight levels must be attained at each level of automobile manufacture, and a desire to succeed in creating automotive excellence must be cultivated in the hearts and minds of all involved.

Editorial Director	Ken Itsuki
Copy Director	Koichi Edagawa
Art Director	Koichi Nonaka
Editorial Supervisors	Teiji Itoh
	Gregory Clark
Art Supervisor	Bernd F. Langer
Translator	Richard Lee
Editorial Assistants	Kimiko Tanaka
	Fusako Matsushita
	Michiyo Kawaike
Interviewers	Takeshi Morita
	Norio Kobiyama
	Toshio Tsuji
	Kenichi Nagata
	Akemi Tanaka
	Noriko Masaki
	Yoshitaka Nonoyama
	Naoko Watanabe
Designers	Shoichi Yabu
	Noriko Wakatsuki
	Mutsumi Iseki
	Yuko Ishiyama
Photographers	Taikichi Irie
	Takashi Kakinuma
	Naoyuki Watanabe
	Mitsugu Hara
	Taisuke Ogawa
	Minoru Akiyama
	Kazuhiko Ohhori
	Shozo Masuda
	Harumi Konishi
	Sadao Hibi
	Hideo Inose
	Manabu Watanabe
	Katsusuke Chiba
	Norio Yoshida
	Hidenori Fukuma
	Tsukasa Tonoshiro
	Katsuhiko Mizuno
	Ryotaro Nakashima
	Motonobu Sato
	Katsuhiro Yamanashi
	Noriyuki Yoshida
	Satoshi Ogawa
Illustrator	Akira Seto
Calligraphers	Shoichi Oimoto
	Toseki Miura

Special thanks are due to many organizations and persons in Japan, for the kind cooperation they extended in furnishing materials and information for the production of this book. Among them, but in no particular order, are:

Imperial Household Agency
Agency for Cultural Affairs
Tokyo National Museum
Tokyo National Museum of Modern Arts
The Japanese Sword Museum
The Kyushu Ceramic Museum
The Paper Museum
Tokyo National University of Fine Arts and Music
Tokai University Information Technology Center
Tokyo National Research Institute of Cultural Properties
Muto Institute of Structural Mechanics
Wajima Urushi Ware Research Institute
Foundation for Protection of Cultural and Touristic Assets of Kyoto City
Wajima Urushi Ware Cooperative Society
The Society for Preservation of Kikusui-hoko
The Nippon Bonsai Association
Japan Broadcast Publishing Co., Ltd.
The Society for Preservation of Japanese Art Swords
Shinjuku New Center Development Council
Yakushi-ji (Temple)
Horyu-ji (Temple)
Toshodai-ji (Temple)
Todai-ji (Temple)
Rokuon-ji (Temple) Kinkaku-ji
Jisho-ji (Temple) Ginkaku-ji
Zuiho-in
Shisen-do
Jikko-in
Kanei-ji (Temple)
Ryoan-ji (Temple)
Kyoto Yuzen Cooperative Association
Nishijin-ori Industrial Association
Kakiemon-yo Workshop
Imaemon-yo Workshop
Chuemon-yo Workshop
Seisen-yo Workshop
Kyocera Corporation
Taisei Construction Co., Ltd.
Shimizu Construction Co., Ltd.
Kajima Corporation
Asahi Shimbun Publishing Company
Kanamori Lacquer Workshop
Benri-do Ltd.
Sasaki Textile Ltd.
Juraku Ltd.
Shin-kenchiku-sha
Nippon Steel Corporation
Hitachi Ltd.
Asahi Glass Co., Ltd.
Sumitomo Electric Industries Ltd.
Sekai Bunka Photo
Uni Photo Press
Nobuo Ogasawara
Jiro Kohara
Nozomu Ikei
Heiro Kitagawa
Shigeyoshi Iwasaki
Katsumi Komori
(NOTE: Though not listed here, the editors extend their gratitude to the many persons introduced in the pages of this book who graciously gave their time and hospitality to our special interviewers.)